Easy Keto Soup Cookbook

Hearty Fat-Burning Keto Soups For Weight Loss And Optimum Health

LUCY FLORES

ISBN-9781073301645

DEDICATION

For Kimberly, Thank you very always being there!

TABLE OF CONTENTS

INTRODUCTION

Many people who have weight concerns and health issues are constantly on the lookout for a diet that will work for them. The challenge is that while there are so many good diets that they can try, most of them, they do not guarantee a long time sustainable result. An effective diet is one that is sustainable and enjoyable. This diet is the ketogenic diet. The keto diet, as it is also known, is a low carb, high fat and moderate protein diet that enables the body burn fat as its main energy source. By restricting carbohydrate to a minimal level, it pushes your body to a state where it begins to break down stored fats into ketones in order to use it as an alternative fuel source.

The body's main source of energy is carbohydrates. It is its most preferred source because it the easiest to convert to energy. But not necessarily the best. Eating too much high carb foods leads to obesity, diabetes, gastrointestinal distress, and other short and long-term diseases. It makes the body produce more glucose than it needs, making you overeat. Although excess glucose is stored in the body, once you eat lots of high-carb foods and your body requires more glucose, it will send a signal to your brain that will make you crave for more sugary things and eat more high- carb laden foods like processed foods, cookies, candies, snacks and the likes, which causes overweight and health -related diseases.

The ketogenic diet deprives the body of its main energy source, carbohydrate. Once you reduce the carb in your food and increase the fats, the body begins to depend on fat as its primary source. It gets the body to produce ketone or ketone bodies from breaking down fatty acids or fats that has been stored in the liver and muscles. The fat burns faster, turns to ketones, and provide your body with the energy it needs and mental alertness your brain requires.

For that to happen, you must limit your daily net carb consumption to 20-25grams. Limiting your sugar and starches enable you to enter into a metabolic state known as ketosis. Your body will no longer depend on carbohydrates for fuel but will start to use fats as its primary source. Adapting to this new course of metabolism will take about 2 weeks. If you want faster progress however, you must be ready to reduce your carb intake to 15 g per day. But if you eat up to 40 grams carb in a day, you are bound to store glycogen in your liver and muscles which will prevent you from attaining ketosis.

It is no all about carbs as well. Fat and protein must be taken into consideration, especially your fat consumption. In the keto diet, the percentage of the calories consumed should come from about 70-75 % fat, 20-25% protein and 5% carbs. Nevertheless, this percentage varies from one person to the other, as it depends on current lean body weight and daily activity levels. Note that ketogenic diet is not an easy diet to begin. Attaining ketosis comes with certain discomforts. At some point, you will experience certain symptoms like headaches, fatigue and sluggishness. This is known as 'keto- flu' and is perfectly normal. It will pass away after a period of time. The keto diet is naturally diuretic. You will be peeing more often. See that you drink lots to water to replenish the electrolyte being passed out as urine.

Do not worry however, Ketosis is perfectly safe for the body. The process of burning fat, instead of glucose is a normal activity for the body. As a matter of fact, our brain only needs between 20-30grams of glucose to function effectively. Ketogenic diet brings you to a state where ketones becomes your body's main energy source- up to 75%. It is a highly effective diet that has stood the test of time and comes with tremendous health benefits. Although the ketogenic diet was initially designed to address epilepsy in children, it is mostly used nowadays to address weight loss, since it lowers appetite and helps to burn excess stored fats. Besides, it also helps to regulate blood sugar levels, lower the risk of type 2 diabetes and heart disease as well as helping to reduce the risk of certain cancers.

It is a very nutritious diet that is based around real foods with lots of vegetable intake, especially leafy greens. it also contain eggs, fish, fatty meats such as lamb, poultry and pork belly as well as dairy products especially grass- fed butter , nuts and seeds. If you are on a keto diet, you will spend more time cooking your own food than eating out, and that is why this book has been written. The recipes in this book will help you look forward to meal times on account of its quick, easy-to- follow, nutritious and mouthwatering ketogenic soup recipes.

The healthy compilation of delicious and satisfying soup dishes will make you and your family look forward to dinner- time every day. Besides being easy to follow, the recipes come with everyday keto ingredients that are within your reach. You will enjoy your meals, attain ketosis and keep at it until you achieve your weight loss and other health goals.

Let's Cook!

POULTRY RECIPES

Turkey Zucchini Meatball Soup

Enjoy a delicious and healthy soup that's flavorful and comforting.

Prep Time: 10 minutes

Cook Time: 25 minutes

Serves: 8

Ingredients

For the meatballs:

1 lb. turkey, ground & not too lean

1 large egg

1/4 cup of almond flour, blanched

1/2 teaspoon of fine grain sea salt

1 teaspoon garlic powder

1 teaspoon onion powder

1 teaspoon poultry seasoning blend

Large pinch of crushed red pepper

1 tablespoon olive oil or avocado oil

For the soup:

2 tablespoons of olive oil or avocado oil

1 medium-sized onion, diced

4 garlic cloves, minced

3 cups kale, chopped roughly

6 cups of chicken bone broth or chicken broth (no-sugar added)

1 bay leaf

2 tsp fresh sage, minced

2 tsp fresh rosemary, minced

3 small-med zucchini, spiralized

Sea salt to taste

Black pepper to taste

Fresh parsley, minced

Directions

1. Add together all the meatball ingredients in a bowl and use slightly wet hands to mix thoroughly. Add a tablespoon of olive oil in a large skillet and heat over medium temperature.

2. Now use wet hands to form the meatball mixture into tiny meatballs of about 1 inch diameter. Add them gently to the hot pan to brown, turning a few times to brown well. Remove and set to one side.

3. Add 2 tablespoons of oil to a large stock pot and heat over medium temperature. Add in the onion, let it cook until tender and then add the garlic and let it cook again for 30 seconds. Now add the kale, stir to coat and then sprinkle with sea salt. Sauté mixture for an additional 2 minutes until softened.

4. Add the broth, herbs and bay leaves and let it boil. Set heat to low and once simmering; add in the meatballs to cook again for about 10 minutes.

5. At the 6-8 minute of cooking, add the zucchini noodles to prevent sogginess. Add salt and pepper as desired. Garnish with fresh parsley. Serve and enjoy!

Nutrition Information Per Serving: Calories: 194kcal; Fat: 9g; Carbohydrates:7g; Protein: 23g

Keto Chicken Soup

This classic chicken soup with lots of healthy vegetables is a satisfying dinner dish on busy weeknights!

Prep Time: 10 minutes

Cook Time: 1 hour

Serves: 8

Ingredients

1 whole chicken, rinsed and cleaned well

4 carrots, chopped

1 Jicama, peeled & cubed to 1"

4 celery stalks, chopped

2 whole onions, chopped

5 garlic cloves, minced

1/2 bunch cilantro

1/2 bunch parsley

1/4 cup kosher salt

1 whole lemon

Directions

1. In a large stock pot, add the rinsed and thoroughly cleaned chicken, together with the onions, cilantro, parsley, carrots, garlic and celery.

2. Fill the pot with cold water until the chicken is covered. Place over medium heat to simmer for an hour. Remove any impurities on the surface with a spoon.

3. Once the 1 hour time elapses, remove from heat and set aside for about 20 minutes. Once cooled, add the cubed jicama. Add parsley and cilantro to garnish and then add salt and pepper as needed.

Nutrition Information Per Serving: Calories: 198kcal; Fat: 10g; Carbohydrate: 3g; Protein: 11g

Coconut chicken soup

Thai Curry Coconut Chicken Soup

Flavor- packed and extremely warming, you'd want to try this chicken soup recipe again and again.

Prep Time: 10 minutes

Cook Time: 30 minutes

Serves: 4

Ingredients

2 tablespoons coconut oil

2 red peppers, seeded & sliced

1 small onion, minced finely

1 tablespoon ginger, grated

3 cloves garlic, grated

1 teaspoon lime zest, grated

1-2 green chili, seeded & minced

1/4 teaspoon ground cumin

Cayenne pepper to taste

2 chicken breasts, diced into small pieces

1 (13.5) oz. cans full fat coconut milk

3/4 cup water

1/2 cup chicken stock

3 teaspoons Swerve or xylitol

2 teaspoons liquid amino

1 1/2 tablespoons fish sauce

2 limes juice

Directions

1. Add the coconut oil to a pan and place over medium heat. Add the slices of pepper and sauté for a few minutes until soft. Remove and reserve for later use.

2. Add more coconut oil to the pan and then add the onion. Cook until translucent for about 5 minutes. Add the ginger, lime zest, garlic, cumin, green chili and cayenne pepper. Cook, with frequent stirring for about 5 minutes until it begins to brown.

3. Now add the chicken and cook until the pinkness disappears. Return the peppers, coconut milk as well as the water, stock, fish sauce, sweetener, lime juice and liquid amino

4. Simmer for 10 to 15 minutes with occasional stir. Taste and adjust seasonings as needed.

5. Enjoy over cauliflower rice, with cilantro and lime wedges.

Nutrition Information Per Serving: Calories: 193kcal; Fat: 26g; Carbohydrate: 6.5g; Protein: 14g

Keto Lemon Chicken Soup

Healthy and simple soup that can be made in the instant pot just for you

Prep Time: 10 minutes

Cook Time: 20 minutes

Serves: 6

Ingredients

2 tablespoons olive oil

1 cup celery, chopped

1 cup onion, chopped

2 tablespoons garlic, minced

2 cups carrots, sliced in pieces

1 teaspoons rosemary, chopped

2 teaspoons pepper

1 teaspoon salt

1 teaspoon thyme

1/4 teaspoon red pepper flakes

4 bay leaves

1 lb. boneless chicken breasts

2 quarts chicken broth

1/4 cup lemon juice

Directions

1 .Slice all vegetables, put instant pot on sauté mode. Add oil in the pan when hot, sauté celery, onions and garlic until soft, about 5 minutes.

2. Add carrot and bay leaves, parmesan cheese rind. Put chicken breasts on the vegetables in instant pot. Cover with chicken broth. Don't put lemon juice in it. Cover instant pot and increase heat to cook for about 13 minutes

3. Remove parmesan cheese, and bay leaves in the broth and discard. Mix in lemon juice. Bring chicken out from the pot and shred in a mixer, return to your instant pot, and then mix thoroughly to combine.

4. Enjoy with zucchini noodles or cooked orzo.

Nutrition Information Per Serving: Calories: 291kcal; Faf7g; Carbohydrate14g; Protein: 18g

Mushroom Soup with Creamy Chicken

Easy soup with comforting and creamy taste

Prep Time: 15 minutes

Cook Time: 15 minutes

Serves: 6

Ingredients

1 tablespoon olive oil

8 ounces boneless chicken thighs, into 1" pieces

2 tablespoons butter

Salt and freshly ground black pepper

3 cloves garlic, shredded

8 ounces cremini mushrooms, sliced

1 onion, chopped

3 carrots, peeled and chopped

2 stalks celery, diced

1/2 teaspoon thyme

1/4 cup flour

4 cups chicken stock

1 bay leaf

2 tablespoons parsley leaves chopped

1 sprig rosemary

2/3 low-fat milk and 1/3 cup heavy cream.

Directions

1. Add olive oil in a large stockpot above an average heat. Put salt and pepper to chicken thighs for season, then add the chicken to stockpot and cook for about 3 minutes. Put aside

2. Let butter dissolve in the stockpot in a low heat. Add mushrooms, onion, garlic, celery and carrot .Stir occasionally until soft, add in thyme and cook all in 5 minutes

3. Whisk in flour until browned. Add chicken stock, chicken thighs, and bay leaf, stirring constantly. Cook until thickened in about 5 minutes.

4. Stir in milk and cream until intensely cooked, in 2 minutes; add salt and pepper to taste as desired

5. Serve hot, garnished with parsley and rosemary.

Nutrition Information Per Serving: Calories: 248.8kcal; Fat12.8g; Carbohydrate 18.1g; Protein: 15.7g

Salsa Chicken Soup

A creamy and easy soup that's gluten free.

Prep Time: 5 minutes

Cook Time: 30 minutes

Serves: 7

Ingredients

1 pound boneless chicken breasts

3 cups low sodium chicken broth

8 ounces cream cheese

12 ounces mild salsa

4 teaspoons taco seasoning mix

1 avocado thinly diced

2 tablespoons chopped parsley

1/2 cup shredded cheddar cheese

Directions

1. Slice the cream cheese into 8 cubes. Put aside and make softer.

2. Add chicken broth, taco seasoning and salsa. Mix to the pressure cooker pot. Stir together until well-mixed.

3. Add chicken breasts to the cooker pot, put some water to submerge. Cover the pot for about 25 minutes at high heat

4. Open the pot and bring out only the chicken breasts to a plate. Add softened cream cheese and 1 cup of hot liquid from the pressure cooker pot in a heatproof bowl. Beat for 1 minute till smooth then add to the pot and stir it in. In a low heat.

5. While boiling shred the chicken and pour to the pot. Stir and cook for 2 minutes

6. Serve with avocado, cilantro, and cheddar cheese as desired

Nutrition Information Per Serving: Calories 310 kcal; *Fat* 20g; *Carbohydrate* 8.5g; *Protein:* 23g

Queso Keto Chicken Soup
Full of flavor and creamy, for chilly nights

Prep Time: 5 minutes

Cook Time: 30 minutes

Serves: 6

Ingredients

2 boneless skinless chicken breast pieces in two

28 ounces tiny diced tomatoes

1/4 teaspoon salt

2 cups chicken broth

1 cup green salsa

2 tablespoons taco seasoning

8 ounces cream cheese very soft

Diced avocado and Monterrey jack cheese for garnish

Directions

1. Put chicken, tomatoes with juices, chicken broth, taco seasoning, salt, and green salsa in instant pot. Turn to manual mode and let it cook for about 10 minutes at high pressure.

2. Let pressure to discharge as you would expect, for about 15 minutes, then take away and pieces the chicken and set aside.

3. Stir the very soft cream cheese into the soup in the instant pot and whisk until fully heated into the soup. Add now the pieced chicken to the soup.

4. Serve with avocado and Monterrey jack cheese.

Nutrition Information Per Serving: Calories 237kcal; *Fat*15g; *Carbohydrate* 14g; *Protein:* 12g

Rice and Creamy Chicken Soup
Comforting and hearty soup with cauliflower to your satisfaction

Prep Time: 5 minutes

Cook Time: 15 minutes

Serves: 1

Ingredients

1/2 tablespoon butter

1/2 cups cooked chicken chopped

1/2 teaspoon chopped garlic

1.5 ounces cauliflower riced

1/2 cup chicken stock

1/4 cup half and half cream

1 sprig rosemary

1/2 cups cooked chicken chopped

Directions

1. Let butter dissolve in pan over medium heat. Add the garlic and cook for about 1 minute. Add the cauliflower and let it fry quickly for about 2 minutes.

2. Mix in the chicken, cream, chicken stock, and rosemary. Cook until the mixture has condensed and begun to thicken, all in 5 minutes.

3. Drain out 1/2 of the riced cauliflower then blend. Take out about 1/2 cup of the soup mixture, and also put the chicken to the boiling soup.

4. Add cream broth to the blended cauliflower and blend until smooth. Put back to the pot with salt and pepper to taste.

5. Heat thoroughly, take rosemary away and discard

6. Serve hot

Nutrition Information Per Serving: Calories 428kcal*; Fa30g; Carbohydrate* 10g*; Protein* 28g

Keto Green Chili Chicken Soup

Flavorful low carb Green Chili Chicken soup, with spices topped with cheese

Prep Time: 10 minutes

Cook Time: 40 minutes

Serves: 8

Ingredients

4 Boneless skinless chicken breasts, trimmed

18 ounces cream cheese, soft

14 ounces green chilies, sliced

1/4 tablespoon cumin

1/4 tablespoon salt

1/4 tablespoon pepper

1/2 tablespoon garlic powder

1 cup Monterey jack cheese, shredded

Directions

1. In a bowl, mix garlic powder, cumin, cream cheese, pepper salt together until well mixed in heated oven (375F). Then add in the green chilies and stir thoroughly

2. In a bowl, put the chicken breast add the green chili also top with the Monterey jack cheese

3. Let it bake on the middle rack for about 45 minutes, see that the chicken is well cooked and the juice submerged

4. Serve hot and enjoy with sautéed spinach can also go with cauliflower rice.

Nutrition Information Per Serving: Calories 253kcal; *Fat* 8g; *Carbohydrate* 2g; *Protein* 26g

Keto Vegetable Chicken Soup

This Keto Vegetable Chicken Soup is delicious and easy, enjoy

Prep Time: 5 minutes

Cook Time: 30 minutes

Serves: 12

Ingredients

1 tablespoon olive oil

2 cups celery, chopped

3 tablespoons ginger, grated

4 garlic cloves, shredded

2 pounds boneless skinless chicken breast

2 quarts chicken broth

3 cups chopped carrots

¼ teaspoon turmeric

3 cups broccoli florets

1 ½ cups frozen peas

¼ cup chopped parsley

1 onion, chopped

½ teaspoon crushed red pepper

Directions

1. Heat olive oil on medium heat. Put celery, onion, garlic, and ginger and cook for 5 minutes until soften

2. Then add in the chicken breast, broth, cider vinegar, turmeric, carrots, and red pepper and let it boil for about 15 minutes for the chicken in it to cook

3. Take the chicken out, chop into small pieces. Put parsley, broccoli, and peas to the soup and boil

4. Add seasonings to taste if needed and the chopped chicken

5. Enjoy!

Nutrition Information Per Serving: Calories 227kcal; *Fat*8.0g; *Carbohydrate* 10.3g; *Protein* 27.5g

Keto White Chili Chicken
Flavored and creamy soup, for you

Prep Time: 5 minutes

Cook Time: 30 minutes

Serves: 6

Ingredients

2 tablespoons olive oil

1 onion, diced

2 teaspoons garlic powder

1/2 teaspoon cayenne

8 cups broth

1 cup salsa verde

1 lb. chicken

2 teaspoons cumin

1/2 teaspoon chili powder

3 avocados

Directions

1. Heat olive oil over medium heat. Cook onion 4 minutes. Put spices, garlic powder, cayenne, chili powder, cook for about 2 minutes

2. Stir in remaining ingredients except avocado and cook for about 20 minutes.

3. Take chicken out, cut into pieces, then ad back to soup. Seasoning well for taste

4. Serve the soup with half (1/2) of one avocado each plate.

Nutrition Information Per Serving: Calories 402kcal*; Fat*29.2g*; Carbohydrate*5.3g*; Protein* 23g

Keto Pumpkin Chicken Soup

Enjoy pumpkin Chicken Soup, healthy and creamy for you

Prep Time: 10 minutes

Cook Time: 20 minutes

Serves: 6

Ingredients

1 cup coconut milk

2 cups chicken bone broth

6 cups baked pumpkin

1 teaspoon garlic powder

1 teaspoon ground cinnamon

1 teaspoon dried ginger

1 teaspoon nutmeg

1 teaspoon paprika

Sea salt and pepper to taste

Directions

1. Add coconut milk, pumpkin, broth, and spices in a heated pan, stir to mix and let it cook for about 15 minutes

2. Blend this mixture in a blender smoothly, if watery, again on low heat until it is thick enough to your satisfaction

3. Top with pumpkin seeds and serve

Nutrition Information Per Serving: Calories 123kcal; *Fat*9.8g; *Carbohydrate* 8.1g; *Protein*3.1g

Keto Wild Rice Chicken Soup

This Keto Wild Rice Chicken Soup very easy to make with gluten free and perfect for winter nights

Prep Time: 5 minutes

Cook Time: 4 hours

Serves: 2

Ingredients

1 lb. skinless boneless chicken breast

3 carrots, diced

1 1/2 cups celery, diced

1 1/2 cups onion, diced

3 garlic cloves, shredded

1 cup wild rice

6 cups of chicken broth

1 tablespoon rosemary, shredded

Salt & pepper to season

1 tablespoon thyme, shredded

2 tablespoons of unsalted butter

2 tablespoons of cornstarch

1 cup whole milk

Directions

1. Add the chicken breast the season with salt and pepper. Then add celery, garlic, rosemary, wild rice, carrots, onion, thyme, and chicken broth. Cook on high heat for 3 hours

2. Take chicken out and shred using fork, then add it back to soup. Melt butter in another pan, once the color is changed to light brown ad milk and corn starch and stir living no lumps. Cook for 2 minutes

3. Add milk mixture into soup and stir. Put mushroom and stir too, cook for about 30 minutes. Season with pepper and salt

4. Enjoy!

Nutrition Information Per Serving: Calories 213kcal*; Fat*5g*; Carbohydrate* 4g*; Protein*17g

Keto Spinach Soup and Chicken Sausage
A pleasing recipe for week night and dinner; eat healthy!

Prep Time: 10 minutes

Cook Time: 15minutes

Serves: 4

Ingredients

2 tablespoons butter

12 ounces cooked Italian-style chicken sausage, sliced

3½ cups chicken bone broth

1 onion, chopped

4 cloves garlic, crushed

1/3 cup heavy whipping cream

6 cups spinach

25

Sea salt, to taste

Red pepper flakes, to taste

Black pepper, to taste

Directions

1. On a medium heat, heat the butter. Add onion and sausage, cook until the sausage and onion is brown softened, for about 8 minutes, stirring occasionally. Then add garlic, cook for 1 minute.

2. Put the bone broth and red pepper flakes and let it boil. Reduce the heat and cover the pot to cook for about 5 minutes.

3. Add the spinach and cook until wilted, constantly stirring and cook for about 2 minutes. Then put off the heat and add the cream

4. For taste add salt, black pepper, and season as desired

5. Serve hot

Nutrition Information Per Serving: Calories 358kcal*; Fat25.7 g; Carbohydrate* 8.2g*; Protein24.2g*

Keto Chicken Broccoli Alfredo Soup (Crock pot)

A Healthy and well -flavored meal. So tasty!

Prep Time: 10 minutes

Cook Time: 6 hours

Serves: 8

Ingredients

1 1/2 lb. boneless skinless chicken breast

8 ounces cream cheese, diced

7 cups broccoli, sliced

2 cups chicken broth

3 cloves garlic, minced

1 cup heavy whipping cream

1 1/2 cup Parmesan cheese, shredded

Salt and pepper

Directions

1. Season chicken breast with salt and pepper in the crock pot, then add all ingredient except Parmesan cheese. Cook for 6 hours on low heat

2. Next, bring out the chicken breast and shred with 2 forks, when shredded, add back to pot.

3. Now add the Parmesan cheese and mix well. Cook for few minutes and turn off heat.

4. Serve hot! And enjoy.

Nutrition Information Per Serving: Calories 376kcal; Fat27g; Carbohydrate 5g; Protein28

FISH AND SEA FOOD RECIPES

Italian Seafood Soup

Delicious and elegant soup, with low carb and gluten free. Enjoy!

Prep Time: 15 minutes

Cook Time: 35 minutes

Serves: 6

Ingredients

3 Tablespoons butter

1 onion diced

3 garlic cloves minced

2 carrots slice

29 ounces diced tomatoes

32 ounces broth low-salt chicken

1 celery stalk sliced

1 Tablespoon dried basil

1/2 teaspoon dried oregano

1 pound shrimp peeled and tail and vein off

1 pound sea scallops

1 pound cod diced

10 clams washed

2 14.5 ounce cans, small diced

10 mussels cleaned, bear removed

1/2 teaspoon dried thyme

3/4 cup white wine

Directions

1. In a medium heat, melt butter and add garlic, carrots, onion, celery, cook for five minutes to soft.

2. Then add tomatoes, chicken broth, basil, wine, oregano, and thyme and stir to mix. Cook for 30 minutes.

3. Add the seafood into the mixture and let it boil. Reduce the heat and simmer for 7 minutes.

4. Add salt to taste, cook until seafood is cooked and clams and mussels are opened.

5. Serve hot.

Nutrition Information Per Serving: Calories 255kcal; *Fat*7g; *Carbohydrate* 16g; *Protein26g*

Keto Shrimp Soup with Vegetables

Hearty and creamy soup with low carb. Enjoy

Prep Time: 10 minutes

Cook Time: 5 hours 30 minutes

Serves: 6

Ingredients

6.5 ounces cauliflower, trimmed to florets

5 ounces broccoli, cut to florets

4 ounces turnip chopped

4 cups vegetable broth

8.5 ounces shrimp frozen

2 bouillon cubes

4 cup water

2 cups heavy cream

Salt to taste

Directions

1. In a crockpot, add all vegetables, chicken broth, and heavy cream. Add little salt and stir to mix properly.

2. Cover to cook for about 4 hours and 30 minutes.

3. Add the shrimps, and cover to cook for another 30 minutes, then add salt to taste. Serve hot.

Nutrition Information Per Serving: Calories 348kcal*; Fat*31g*; Carbohydrate* 6g*; Protein*11g

Keto Salmon Soup

Healthy soup that warms you up in a cold day

Prep Time: 5 minutes

Cook Time: 30 minutes

Serves: 4

Ingredients

2 tablespoon butter

1 daikon radish, peeled and chopped

4 skinless salmon fillets chopped

½ cup heavy cream

2 tablespoon chopped fresh dill

½ cup white wine

Salt and black pepper

4 cups seafood stock

1 onion, sliced

Directions

1. In a large pan, melt butter and add onion. Cook for 2 minutes.

2. Put some white wine, and boil well under medium heat. Add daikon and seafood stock. Cook until radish is tender.

3. Add salmon, then heavy cream and dill. Taste for seasoning, pepper, and salt as needed.

4. Serve immediately.

Nutrition Information Per Serving: Calories 473kcal*; Fat29g; Carbohydrate* 5g*; Protein39*g

Keto Garlic Butter Shrimp Scampi Soup

So quick, so easy. Soup best for you

Prep Time: 5 minutes

Cook Time: 10 minutes

Serves: 4

Ingredients

2 Tablespoons olive oil

4 tablespoons butter

1 1/4 pounds (600 grams) large shrimp prawns, tails and shell off

1/4 cup white wine

2 tablespoons lemon juice

1/4 cup chopped parsley

5 garlic cloves, crushed

Black pepper

Red pepper flakes

Salt to taste

Directions

1. Heat olive oil in a pan, add two tablespoon of butter, and garlic. Cook for about 2 minutes.

2. Put shrimp and season with salt and pepper. Then cook for 2minutes and turn over the shrimp.

3. Add the white wine and red pepper flakes. Simmer for about 3 minutes or until shrimp is cooked through.

4. Add up remaining butter, parsley, and lemon juice. Then turn off heat.

5. Serve with pasta, garlic bread, or steamed vegetables. To your taste.

Nutrition Information Per Serving: Calories 291kcal; *Fat*13g; *Carbohydrate* 2g; *Protein*35g

Keto Thai Coconut Shrimp Soup
Tasty and creamy to your taste

Prep Time: 5 minutes

Cook Time: 10 minutes

Serves: 4

Ingredients

1 lb. shrimp, vein off and peeled

2 cup of chicken broth

1 tablespoon garlic, crushed

1 tablespoon fish sauce

1 teaspoon chili paste

1/4 cup basil leaves, chopped

1/4 cup cilantro, chopped

1 1/4oz can coconut milk

1 stalk lemongrass, pieced

1 tablespoon fresh lime juice

1 ounce mushrooms, sliced

Directions

1. On high heat, add coconut milk, ginger, broth, and lemon grass in a pot.

2. Add mushroom, fish sauce, chili paste, and lime juice. Reduce heat and cook well until mushrooms are soft, for about 7 minutes.

3. Put shrimp and cook for about 3 minutes to cook through.

4. Enjoy and serve with basil and cilantro.

Nutrition Information Per Serving: Calories240kcal*; Fat*15g*; Carbohydrate* 4g*; Protein32g*

Keto England Seafood Soup
Delicious and healthy soup, for your consumption.

Prep Time: 30minutes

Cook Time: 15 minutes

Serves: 5

Ingredients

1 tablespoon avocado oil

1 tablespoon garlic chopped

¾ teaspoon dry thyme

½ teaspoon salt

¼ teaspoon pepper, preferably white pepper

¼ teaspoon fennel seeds

½ cup white wine dry

2 8-ounce bottles clam juice lower sodium

2 ½ cups chicken broth, divided

4 red potatoes, cut into cubes

1/3 cup flour

8 ounces Alaskan cod, sliced into pieces

½ cup half-and-half

1 onion, chopped

1 pound raw shucked clams

1 cup celery chopped

Nutmeg pinch

Parsley for garnish

Directions

1. On medium heat, add oil in a large pot, when hot put onion, garlic, celery, fennel, thyme, pepper, salt, and nutmeg. Mix severally and cook for about 8 minutes.

2. Then add wine and increase heat. Cook until liquid reduces, for about 4 minutes. Now add juice, potatoes, 2 cups of chicken broth, and cover lid to simmer.

3. Reduce heat to medium, open lid and stir severally till potatoes are soft. Cook for 10 minutes.

4. Add the remaining hair chicken broth and flour. Mix well while cooking, until it becomes thick.

5. Put clams, juice, and cod. Let it cook and stir it rarely. Cook until cod is not vividly seen for about 5 minutes, then stir in half and half and turn off heat.

6. Enjoy soup with chives or parsley.

Nutrition Information Per Serving: Calories 349kcal; *Faf7g; Carbohydrate* 41g; *Protein25*

Keto Shrimp and Bacon Soup

Yummy keto shrimp and bacon soup filled with flavor and comforting taste

Prep Time: 5 minutes

Cook Time: 20 minutes

Serves: 6

Ingredients

1 lb. shrimp vein off peeled and chopped

1/2 lb. bacon

3 cups chicken stock

2 teaspoon paprika smoked

1/4 cup onion chopped

2 teaspoon pink Himalayan salt

2 teaspoon ground black pepper

1 1/2 cups heavy whipping cream

Directions

1. Cook bacon in a pot until crunchy. Pour out in bowl, let it cool and pound.

2. Put onion in a pot, add bacon grease then let it boil. Add heavy whipping cream, chicken stock, pepper, salt, and paprika. Then cook for about 15 minutes until it becomes thick.

3. Put shrimp and pounded bacon, then boil for about 5 minutes.Enjoy!

Nutrition Information Per Serving: Calories405kcal*; Fat29g; Carbohydrate 3g; Protein32g*

Keto Stress-Free Clam Chowder Soup

Rich and hearty meal, so tasty!

Prep Time: 10 minutes

Cook Time: 20 minutes

Serves: 6

Ingredients

5 slices bacon, chopped

1 cup chicken broth

1 onion chopped

1 cup Unsweetened Almond Milk

1 cup Heavy Cream

3 cups cauliflower florets

4 ounces cream cheese

18 ounces canned clams, chopped and drained

2 cloves garlic, crumbled

1 bay leaf

Dried Thyme

Directions

1. Add the chopped bacon in a large pot over medium heat, cook until soft. Then remove bacon from pot and set aside. Leave 3 tablespoon of the bacon drippings in the pot.

2. Put garlic and onion in the pot, cook for 3 minutes. Add thyme and cook for 1 minutes.

3. Put almond milk, chicken broth, cream, cream cheese and stir well until cheese is melted.

4. Put bay leaf, cauliflower florets, and clams. Let it boil in a low heat, cover and cook for 10 minutes.

5. Topped with the cooked bacon when served. Enjoy!

Nutrition Information Per Serving: Calories339kcal*; Fat25g; Carbohydrate* 8g*; Protein*19g

Keto Paella Seafood
Delicious and tasty, eat healthy!

Prep Time: 20 minutes

Cook Time: 20 minutes

Serves: 6

Ingredients

2 (300g) skinless chicken thighs, small pieces

350 g Argentinian Red Shrimps, peeled

130 g scallops

170 g clams

100 g green beans, stems off

1 1/4 teaspoon black pepper

1/2 cup tomato can, diced

1/2 cup chicken stock

4 tablespoon olive oil

2 tablespoon chopped parsley

620 g cauliflower riced

100g onion, diced

3 garlic cloves, minced

1/2 teaspoon turmeric powder

1/2 teaspoon thyme

1 1/4 teaspoon salt

Directions

1. Add chicken, 1 teaspoon of turmeric powder, garlic, thyme, salt and pepper in a bowl, mix well and leave it for few minutes to marinate.

2. In a pot on medium heat, add 2 tablespoon of olive oil and the diced onion, with riced cauliflower. Cook for few minutes and set aside.

3. Add the remaining 2 tablespoon Olive oil in a pot, put the chicken and cook for 2 minutes. Add it up to the cauliflower and stir.

3. Put the saffron threads, chicken broth, diced tomato can, salt and pepper and the shrimps, clams, scallops and green beans. Cover and let the seafood cook for about 5 minutes.

4. Open and bring out the seafood and green beans, put in a bowl and set aside. Cook the soup for 4 minutes while stirring continuously. When the liquid has dried up, add seafood back to pot. Then stem for few minutes and turn off heat.

5. Ready to enjoy!

Nutrition Information Per Serving: Calories388kcal; *Fat*18.81g; *Carbohydrate*13.92g; *Protein*40.57g

Keto Cheesy Shrimp Soup

Easy and healthy soup for you.

Prep Time: 5 minutes

Cook Time: 15 minutes

Serves: 8

Ingredients

1/2 Cup Butter

24oz Extra Small Shrimp

32oz Chicken Broth

2 cups of Sliced Mushrooms

8oz Cheddar Cheese Shredded

1 Cup Heavy Whipping Cream

Directions

1. In a pot on high heat, boil chicken broth and mushroom.

2. Then reduce heat, and add heavy whipping cream, cheese, and butter. Stir well until finally melted.

3. Season and cook shrimp in a different pot, when properly cooked, add to soup. When simmer, turn off heat

4. Garnish soup with parsley if desired. Enjoy!

Nutrition Information Per Serving: Calories451kcal*; Fat33g; Carbohydrate4g; Protein29g*

Keto Creamy Fish Chowder

Healthy soup with tasty ingredient, for you!

Prep Time: 15 minutes

Cook Time: 30 minutes

Serves: 4

Ingredients

1 1/2 pounds haddock, fresh and cut into pieces

1 cup chicken broth

1/4 teaspoon sweet paprika

1 1/2 cups potatoes, peeled and diced

3/4 cup carrots, chopped

1 onion, chopped

4 cup carrots, diced

2 tablespoons butter

2 tablespoons all-purpose flour

2 cups milk

Parsley to garnish

1/2 teaspoon salt

Dash ground black pepper

Directions

1. Add the chicken broth, potatoes, carrots, and seasonings in a pot. Cover and cook until soft for about 8 minutes. Open and put fish and cook for about 8 minutes again. (Set aside)

2. Add butter in a pan on medium heat, add onion and stir fry for about 2 minutes. Then add the flour and stir until well mixed.

3. Put the milk slowly, and stir well until thickened, then add it up to the cooked vegetables and fish that was set aside; continue cooking for about 10 minutes, stirring often. Garnish soup with fresh chopped parsley.

4. Serve hot and enjoy!

Nutrition Information Per Serving: Calories448kcal*; Fat*14g*; Carbohydrate*35g*; Protein*43g

Keto Creamy Shrimp and Corn Soup
It's creamy but not fattening. You will like the taste.

Prep Time: 15 minutes

Cook Time: 30 minutes

Serves: 8

Ingredients

1 pound medium shrimp, peeled and vein off

1/4 cup margarine

10.75oz can condensed cream of chicken soup

10.75oz can low-fat cream of celery soup

16oz package frozen corn kernels

14.5oz can chicken broth

1 cup skim milk

1 onion, sliced

Dried rosemary and thyme

Nutmeg, salt, and pepper to taste.

Directions

1. Add margarine in a large pot on a medium heat, add the shrimps and onion and cook until tender for about 5 minutes.

2. Add the cream of celery soup, cream of chicken soup, corn, milk, broth, rosemary, nutmeg, thyme, salt and pepper to taste. Moderate heat to low and simmer for 20 minutes.

3. Serve hot with French bread or any of your choice.

Nutrition Information Per Serving: Calories231kcal; *Fat*19.9g; *Carbohydrate*21.6g; *Protein*15.7g

Keto French Bouillabaisse
To enjoy seafood, you've got to try this

Prep Time: 20 minutes

Cook Time: 50 minutes

Serves: 4

Ingredients

½ Pound Shrimp, peeled and shell reserved

12 full Black Peppercorns

3 Tablespoons Extra Virgin Olive Oil

½ Teaspoon Kosher Salt

2 Small Fennel Bulbs, sliced, fronds kept

1 Leek, white part only, sliced

4 Cloves Garlic, shredded

4 Tomatoes, seeds and skins detached and chopped

1 Cup White Wine, dry

1 Teaspoon Marjoram, fresh

½ Teaspoon Saffron Threads

½ Teaspoon Ground Cayenne Pepper

½ Pound Sockeye Salmon, skin removed, cut

½ Pound Cod,

½ Pound Manila Clams

½ Pound Bay Mussels

1 Teaspoon Thyme, fresh

6 Cups Water

1 Bay Leaf

1 Onion, diced

Peel from 1 Orange

Directions

1. Boil the 6 cups of water in a pot, add shrimp shells, peppercorns, orange peel and bay leaf and boil in a low heat for about 15 minutes. Put aside

2. Heat the oil in another pan, put leek, onion, fennel bulb, and salt. Let them steam for about 20 minutes

3. Then add garlic and let garlic become soft, stir in the wine and tomato. Increase the heat and allow wine boil well and reduce a bit

4. Pour the orange and shrimp stock that was set aside into this onion mixture. Add the thyme, saffron, cayenne and marjoram, boil for about 10 minutes.

5. Ten put fish, after some minutes later, add clams and mussels. Then cook for 2 minutes before you add the shrimp. Give it two minutes to cook or when shrimp is well cooked, then you turn off heat.

6. Serve and garnish with left fennel fronds. Enjoy!

Nutrition Information Per Serving: Calories448kcal; Fat18g; Carbohydrate18g; Protein47g

Thai Hot and Sour Shrimp Soup
Tasty soup, healthy looks!

Prep Time: 15 minutes

Cook Time: 45 minutes

Serves: 4

Ingredients

1 lb. shrimp, vein off, tail on and peeled

2 tablespoon coconut oil, dived into two

1 inch ginger root, peeled and slice

1 inch lemongrass stalk, roughly chopped

1 inch red Thai chilies, roughly chopped

5 cups chicken broth

1/2 lb. button mushrooms, washed and sliced

1 small green zucchini

2 tablespoon fresh lime juice

2 tablespoon fish sauce

1/4 bunch fresh Thai basil, chopped

1/2 tsp fresh lime zest

1 onion, chopped

4 garlic cloves

1/4 bunch cilantro, chopped

Salt, to taste

Pepper to taste

Directions

1. Heat up the first half of the coconut oil, put shrimp shells and stir often not burn and cook well until they are red in colors.

2. Put garlic, onion, ginger, lime zest, chilies, lemongrass, salt and pepper. Cook until onions are soft for about 3 minutes, then stir in chicken broth. Boil for 30 minutes.

3. Then drain the shrimp stock, remove shell, and put stock back on stove to boil on low heat. While boil heat up the other half coconut oil in another pan, add zucchini, and mushroom with a pinch of salt and pepper. Cook through and pour into the shrimp broth.

4. Then add the raw shrimp, let it boil for about 2 minutes, stir in fish sauce, lime juice, salt, pepper, and seasoning to taste. Let shrimp cook well for about 2 minutes.

5. Serve with basil and cilantro.

Nutrition Information Per Serving: Calories249kcal*; Fat*14g*; Carbohydrate*7.6g*; Protein*25.7g

Keto Mexican Shrimp Soup

So comforting and healthy. Try this!

Prep Time: 5 minutes

Cook Time: 30 minutes

Serves: 6

Ingredients

1/4 cup olive oil

2 carrots, cut

2 celery stalks, cut

2 tablespoon tomato paste with chilies

1 15- ounce can diced tomatoes

2 packets of Goya sazon (tomato & cilantro included)

1 teaspoon of Mexican oregano, dried

1.5-2 lb. large shrimp (peeled, deveined with peels set aside)

1 large onion, sliced

8 cups vegetable broth

5 cloves garlic, sliced

1 teaspoon black pepper

Lime wedges

Cilantro

Chopped Avocado

Sliced jalapeños

Directions

1. In a pot, add olive oil, shrimps shell with a bit of salt. Cover lid and let it bake on medium heat for about 5 minutes.

 2. Open and pour a cup of water and scrub the bottom of the pot to get the bits that came out of the shells, stir well and bring out shells.

3. Put onions, carrots, garlic, garlic, celery, jalapeno and tomato paste. Let it steam on medium heat with cover on for about 5 minutes.

4. Put black pepper, Mexican oregano, canned tomatoes, Goya seasoning, and vegetable broth. Boil for about 20 minutes. Then add shrimp, simmer for about 5 minutes, taste for seasoning.

5. Serve and garnish with Lime wedges, cilantro, chopped Avocado, sliced jalapeños and diced onion.

Nutrition Information Per Serving: Calories248kcal*; Fat*10g*; Carbohydrate*13g*; Protein*24g

VEGETABLE RECIPES

Keto Vegetable Soup Instant Pot

Filling soup. Tasty

Prep Time: 10 minutes

Cook Time: 12 minutes

Serves: 6

Ingredients

1 tablespoons olive oil

2 celery stalks, sliced

1.5 cups zucchini, chopped

3 cups cabbage, chopped

1 15 oz. can red kidney beans, drained

1 15 oz. can tomatoes, diced

4 cups low sodium vegetable

1 teaspoon Italian seasoning

1/2 teaspoon ground paprika

1/2 teaspoon black pepper

1/2 teaspoon salt

1 tablespoon lemon juice

1/4 teaspoon cayenne pepper

5 garlic cloves, shredded

1 onion, sliced

5 mushrooms, sliced

2 cups cauliflower florets

2 carrots, chopped

1/2 teaspoon turmeric

1 bay leaf

Directions

1. Put olive oil in the pot, let heat up for 2 minutes. Add onion and stir continuously, put mushrooms and sauté for 2 minutes.

2. Then add, celery, garlic, cabbage, red kidney beans, can tomatoes, vegetable, lemon juice, cauliflower florets and carrots. Mix well

3. Put the Italian seasoning, turmeric, cayenne pepper and bay leaf. Cover and press "soup" setting and time to 12 minutes.

4. Season with salt and pepper to taste. Then when cooked put off and let it cool.

5. Enjoy!

Nutrition Information Per Serving: Calories170kcal; *Fat*4g; *Carbohydrate*26g; *Protein*10g

Keto Meatball and Vegetable Soup
Healthy and satisfying soup, full of veggies and protein

Prep Time: 20 minutes

Cook Time: 45 minutes

Serves: 6

<u>Ingredients</u>

20oz turkey

1/4 cup whole wheat breadcrumbs

1/4 cup grated parmesan cheese

1 egg

2 teaspoon olive oil

2 onions

1 cup diced carrots

1/2 cup diced celery

3garlic cloves, minced

1 can tomatoes, diced

6 cups organic chicken broth

2 bay leaves

1 cup parsley, chopped

Kosher salt and fresh ground black pepper

Salt and fresh ground pepper to taste

<u>Directions</u>

1. Put turkey, breadcrumbs, parsley, egg, onion, salt, garlic and cheese in a large bowl. Mix it together using your hands, and roll into meatballs.

2. Put your baking pan in the oven heated to 400°F, spray oil and place balls. Bake for about 20 minutes and set aside.

3. On high heat, heat olive oil in a pot. When hot turn heat to medium and add onion, celery, carrot, and garlic. Boil for about 15 minutes.

4. Put tomatoes, bay leaves, broth, salt and pepper. Let it boil. After 15 minutes remove bay leaves and put the meatballs. Let it cook for 10 minutes.

5. Serve and garnish with parmesan and chopped parsley.

Nutrition Information Per Serving: Calories252kcal*; Fat*9g*; Carbohydrate*14g*; Protein*39g

Keto Healthy Creamy Vegetable Soup
Creamy soup with low calorie, super tasty

Prep Time: 15 minutes

Cook Time: 35 minutes

Serves: 6

Ingredients

700g head of cauliflower, diced

1000 g zucchinis, peeled and sliced

500 ml vegetable broth

500 ml water

250 ml milk, no fat

1/2 teaspoon garlic powder

1/2 onion powder

1 tablespoon olive oil

3 garlic clove, crumbled

2 onions, chopped

2 large carrots, chopped

3 celery sticks, sliced

2 red capsicum, sliced

1 teaspoon dried thyme

Black pepper

Salt and pepper

Directions

1. Put cauliflower in a pot, add 1 onion, 500g zucchini, 1 garlic cloves, vegetable broth and water. Cover pot and boil for about 15 minutes.

2. Pour into a blender, add onion and garlic powder, milk and pepper, and blend. Set broth aside.

3. Add oil to pot, put the garlic and onion left, sauté for 1 minute. Add celery and carrot and cook for about 2 minutes.

3 Then add the remaining zucchini, thyme, and capsicum. Cook until softened, about 2 minutes. Stir in broth and add water for your desired thickness. Add salt and pepper to taste.

4. Serve and garnish with parsley if desired.

Nutrition Information Per Serving: Calories124kcal*; Fat6g; Carbohydrate9g; Protein20g*

Keto Spaghetti Vegetable Soup

Prep Time: 15 minutes

Cook Time: 35 minutes

Serves: 6

Ingredients

1 Spaghetti crush, baked

4 tablespoon virgin olive oil

1 gallon of vegetable broth

1 Red bell pepper, cut

1 Green bell pepper, cut

2 tablespoon Salt to taste

Black pepper to taste

1 Bunch of kale, chopped

1 Onion, sliced

Directions

1. On a low heat, add oil to pot and fry onion until brown, add kale and pepper. Stir fry for 7 minutes.

2. Put vegetable broth and increase heat to medium. Boil for about 30 minutes. Put the baked Spaghetti in the soup and add the sprig of rosemary. Simmer for 7minutes.

3. Your tasty Spaghetti Vegetable Soup is ready. Enjoy

Nutrition Information Per Serving: Calories200kcal; *Fat*10g; *Carbohydrate*24g; *Protein*2g

Keto Diet Chicken and Vegetable Soup

Simple soup with healthy taste, makes you ask for more

Prep Time: 10 minutes

Cook Time: 30 minutes

Serves: 8

Ingredients

2 tablespoons olive oil

2 shoots celery, cut

2 carrots, cut

2 cloves garlic, shredded

6 cups chicken broth

1 zucchini, sliced

1 can diced tomatoes

2 chicken breasts, boneless and skinless

1 yellow bell pepper, chopped

1 onion, chopped

2 cups spinach, chopped

2 cups cauliflower florets

Salt and pepper, to taste

Directions

1. Put olive oil in a pot on medium heat, add onion, carrots, bell pepper, and celery. Boil until brown for about 5 minutes.

2. Add garlic, chicken broth, cauliflower, tomatoes, and zucchini, boil for 2minutes.

3. Put chicken breasts, salt and pepper to taste, and cook on low heat with cover on for 25 minutes.

4. Take chicken breasts out and shred with two forks, and add back to pot.

5. Enjoy soup

Nutrition Information Per Serving: Calories216kcal*; Fat*8.9 g*; Carbohydrate*12g*; Protein*22.4 g

Detox soup

Keto Detox Green Soup

Healthy and refreshing soup. This is for you

Prep Time: 10 minutes

Cook Time: 15 minutes

Serves: 4

Ingredients

2 1/2 Large Handful baby spinach

1 cup parsley, sliced

2 cups cauliflower florets

Onion medium size, chopped

1/2 teaspoon ginger, grated

2 cups Vegetable stock

1 tablespoon coconut cream

Salt and pepper to taste

1 tablespoon Cooking fat of your choice

Directions

1. In a pot on medium heat, add the cooking fat of your choice, when hot, reduce heat and add heat ad a little salt, when brown add cauliflower florets, let it boil until softened.

2. Put vegetable stock, cover pot and increase heat to boil. When vegetables are soft, add flat parsley, coconut cream, and baby spinach. Stir and boil for 2 minutes.

3. Then blend in a blender until smooth. Soup is ready.

Nutrition Information Per Serving: Calories88kcal*; Fat*6.2g*; Carbohydrate*7g*; Protein*2g

Keto Japanese Onion Soup With Vegetable Broth

Flavored and tasty soup! You need to try this

Prep Time: 10 minutes

Cook Time: 30 minutes

Serves: 4

Ingredients

2 onions, sliced

1 handful button mushrooms, sliced

6 cups vegetable broth

2 carrots, peeled and diced

2 garlic cloves, chopped

2 celery stalks, sliced

1 handful scallions, sliced

Soy sauce

Salt and pepper

Directions

1. Fry onion with a little oil in a pot until brown, then put celery, carrot, garlic and vegetable broth.

2. Let it boil for about 30 minutes, and add salt and pepper to taste.

3. After some minutes, drain the vegetables from the broth, add scallions and mushrooms.

4. Turn off heat, serve and add soy sauce. Enjoy!

Nutrition Information Per Serving: Calories100kcal; Fat2.2g; Carbohydrate10.9g; Protein8.9g

Keto Low-Carb Mushroom Soup with Vegetable Broth

Easy, healthy, and creamy soup for you

Prep Time: 10 minutes

Cook Time: 10 minutes

Serves: 4

Ingredients

55g butter

400g mushrooms, sliced

500ml vegetable stock

250ml heavy cream

1 spring onion, sliced

1scallion, sliced

1 clove garlic, shredded

Directions

1. Heat the butter and fry onion, mushrooms, and garlic in a pot for about 5 minutes.

2. Take small mushrooms out to garnish later, add the vegetable stock to the remaining fried onions, mushrooms and garlic in the pot. Mix well and cook for about 5 minutes again.

3. Turn off heat and blend smoothly. Add cream and cook on low heat for just 2 minutes.

4. Serve and spray a few cream, and mushrooms for garnish. You can enjoy with some low-carb bread if desired.

Nutrition Information Per Serving: Calories333kcal; *Fat*33.3g; *Carbohydrate*6.6g; *Protein*4.9g

Keto Healthy Bacon and Vegetables Soup

Prep Time: 7 minutes

Cook Time: 25 minutes

Serves: 6

Ingredients

2 oz. bacon, diced

500 g vegetables

20 g olive oil

2 tablespoons stock concentrate

1000g water

140g tomato paste

1 onion, sliced

2 garlic cloves, skinned

Parsley, chopped

Black pepper

Lemon zest, grated

Directions

1. Put oil and bacon a pot, cook for about 5 minutes on high heat.

2. Put stock concentrated, water, vegetables, tomato paste and black pepper.

3. Let it cook for 13 minutes. Turn off heat. Serve and enjoy with parsley and lemon zest.

Nutrition Information Per Serving: Calories136kcal*; Fat4.9g; Carbohydrate12.5g; Protein7.6g*

Keto Beef Quinoa and Vegetable Soup: Slow Cooker

So nourishing, with Quinoa that contain all nine essential amino acids.

Prep Time: 15 minutes

Cook Time: 8 hours

Serves: 14

Ingredients

1 1/2 lbs. of beef

2 tablespoon olive oil

4 cups beef stock

1 cup green beans

2 carrots, chopped

1/2 cup quinoa

2 tablespoon Worcestershire sauce

1 onion, chopped

2 ribs celery, sliced

1 tomato, chopped

3 cloves garlic, shredded

1 teaspoon sea salt

1 teaspoon black pepper

Directions

1. Set slow cooker on low heat, fry beef in olive oil until brown, then add to slow cooker.

2. Put beef stock, celery, carrot, green beans, garlic, onion, tomato, Worcestershire sauce, quinoa, pepper and salt.

3. Place lid and cook on low for about 8 hours.

4. Enjoy healthy soup

Nutrition Information Per Serving: Calories125kcal*; Fat*5.5g*; Carbohydrate*8g*; Protein*10g

Keto Zesty Cabbage Soup
Tasty and delicious soup with low calories. You will enjoy this

Prep Time: 10 minutes

Cook Time: 20 minutes

Serves: 6

Ingredients

1 tablespoon olive oil

3 1/2 cup broth, vegetables

¼ tablespoon red pepper flakes

1 teaspoon dried oregano

1 teaspoon dried basil

1 bay leaf

1/2 head green cabbage, shredded

1/2 cup tomato puree

1 onion, chopped

1 carrot, cut

3 garlic cloves, crushed

1/3 cup fresh parsley, sliced

1 cup celery, chopped

Salt and pepper, to taste

Directions

1. Put olive oil in a pot, when hot add onion and bell pepper, cook for 3minutes.

2. Stir in carrot, garlic, celery, spices and a pinch of salt. Let it cook for another 3minutes.

3. Put bay leaf, tomato puree, broth, and cabbage. Boil and reduce heat, cook for 20 minutes

.4. Add parsley, pepper and salt to taste.

5. Serve and squash some fresh lemon in it if desired. Enjoy!

Nutrition Information Per Serving: Calories67kcal; *Fat*2.6 g; *Carbohydrate*10.8 g; *Protein*1.9 g

Keto Hamburger Vegetable Soup

Comforting and Hearty soup. You would ask for more

Prep Time: 10 minutes

Cook Time: 20 minutes

Serves: 10

Ingredients

1 tablespoon olive oil

1 pound ground beef

1 1/2 ounces of diced onion

1 1/2 ounces green pepper, sliced

1/2 ounce celery, cut

32 ounces chicken stock

1 14-ounces can diced tomatoes and chilies

1 teaspoon of salt

1/2 teaspoon garlic powder

1 teaspoon cider vinegar

1 pinch of stevia powder

5 ounce of cabbage, cut

Water

Directions

1. Fry ground beef in oil, put onion, celery, chicken stock, green pepper, and tomatoes. Cook until soft.

2. Add salt, garlic powder, stevia, cabbage, and vinegar. Then cook for 20 minutes (make sure cabbage is soft).

3. Put water as desired to make soup not to thick.

4. Enjoy!

Nutrition Information Per Serving: Calories121kcal; Fat4g g; Carbohydrate6g; Protein12 g

Keto Thai Coconut Milk soup with Veggies
Spicy soup that calms the nerves

Prep Time: 10 minutes

Cook Time: 25 minutes

Serves: 4

Ingredients

1 tablespoon oil, divided.

3 cups cabbage, shredded

2 stalks lemongrass, pieces

1/2 teaspoon ground curry

1 teaspoon garlic, crushed

1 3/4 cups coconut milk

5 cups vegetable stock

2 tablespoon lime juice, divided

1 tablespoon red chili paste

2 Thai bird eyes red peppers, sliced

Black pepper

Salt to taste

Cilantro

Sliced lime

Directions

1. Heat up oil in a large pot add cabbage, 1 tablespoon lime juice, pepper, and 1 teaspoon garlic. Cook on medium high for about 2 minutes. Set aside when cooked.

2. Boil broth, lemon grass, and all spice. Cook for 10 minutes on low heat.

3. Add cabbage that was set aside to broth, lime juice, and coconut milk. Stir and simmer for about 10 minutes.

4. Serve and garnish with Thai Red peppers

Nutrition Information Per Serving: Calories244kcal*; Fat*16g*; Carbohydrate*13g*; Protein*3 g

Keto Spicy Carrot Soup

Delicious soup for dinner. You won't regret cooking!

Prep Time: 10 minutes

Cook Time: 40 minutes

Serves: 8

Ingredients

1 tablespoon butter

1 stalk celery, chopped

2 cloves garlic, chopped

1 teaspoon chopped

5 cups carrots, chopped

2 cups water

1 onion, sliced

4 cups less sodium vegetable broth

Salt to taste

Parsley

Ground pepper to taste

Directions

1. Over medium heat, add butter to pot. When melted put onion, and celery; stir and cook for about 6 minutes.

2. Put parsley and garlic, stir and cook for about 10 seconds. Add carrot, water, and vegetable broth.

3. Cook until tender for about 25 minutes then blend smoothly.

4. Add salt and pepper to taste then serve.

Nutrition Information Per Serving: Calories176kcal; *Fat*18 g; *Carbohydrate*22 g; *Protein*7 g

Keto Low Carb Easy Broccoli Soup

So creamy! Super easy soup for you

Prep Time: 10 minutes

Cook Time: 30 minutes

Serves: 4

Ingredients

2 cups vegetable stock

3 cups celery, sliced

3 cups broccoli florets, sliced

1 can, full-fat coconut milk

1/2 teaspoon onion powder

1/2 teaspoon garlic pepper

Salt, and red pepper flakes pepper to taste

Directions

1. Put celery, broccoli, stock, onion powder, coconut milk, garlic pepper, and red pepper flakes in a pot.

2. Cook for about 30 minutes until soft.

3. Then blend smoothly. Add back to pot and add salt and pepper to taste.

4. Soup is ready. Enjoy!

Nutrition Information Per Serving: Calories200kcal; *Fat*17g; *Carbohydrate*5g; *Protein*4g

BEEF AND LAMB SOUP

Keto Beef Vegetable Soup

This soup is tasty and healthy. You will enjoy it

Prep Time: 10 minutes

Cook Time: 35 minutes

Serves: 6

Ingredients

2 tablespoons extra virgin olive oil, shared

1 1/2 pounds bone-in beef, short ribs

1 cup zucchini, chopped

6 cups beef broth, shared

1 cup carrots, chopped

1/2 cup onion, chopped

2 cups red cabbage, sliced

2 tablespoons tomato paste

1 cup red bell peppers, chopped

1 teaspoon salt

2 bay leaves

1/2 teaspoon black pepper

2 tablespoons parsley, chopped

Directions

1. Put short ribs in the heated oil and fry until brown on medium heat. Add short ribs to instant pot with 2 cups beef broth cook for about 35 minutes.

2. Put olive oil in a soup pot, add carrots, onion, and red bell pepper and cook well for about 4 minutes. Then add red cabbage and zucchini, let it cook for about 3 minutes.

3. Add to the soup the 4 cups beef broth left, with bay leaves, tomato paste, salt and pepper. Let it boil and simmer for about 10 minutes then remove bay leaves.

4. On instant pot, turn off heat, remove bones from short ribs and shred meat using two forks. Add meat and broth used to cook the meat to soup and simmer.

5. Serve and garnish with parsley

Nutrition Information Per Serving: Calories626kcal*; Fat*49g*; Carbohydrate*10g*; Protein*28g

Keto Beef and Lamb Soup
Enjoy this comforting soup cooked on slow cooker.

Prep Time: 50minutes

Cook Time: 8-1/2 hours

Serves: 12

Ingredients

1 1/2 cup beef broth

1/2 cup olive oil

6 cups hot cooked brown rice

16 ounces kidney beans

1 pound beef stew meat, cut

1 pound lamb stew meat, cut

1-1/2 teaspoons dried thyme, separated

1-1/4 teaspoons dried marjoram, separated

3/4 teaspoon dried rosemary, crushed and separated

3/4 teaspoon pepper, separated

10 small red potatoes, cut up in halves

1/2 pound medium fresh mushrooms, cut up in halves

2 medium onions, sliced

2 cups fresh cauliflower florets

1-1/2 cups fresh green beans, cut

3 medium carrots, cut

4 garlic cloves, minced and separated

1 celery rib, sliced

2 tablespoons parsley, minced

1-1/2 teaspoons salt, separated

2 teaspoons sugar

3 tablespoons cornstarch

1/4 cup cold water

Directions

1. Add ½ cup of broth, oil, 1/2 teaspoon salt, 2 minced garlic cloves, 3/4 teaspoon marjoram, 1/2 teaspoon rosemary, 1/4 teaspoon pepper, 1 teaspoon thyme, beef and lamb in a plastic bag with seal. Seal, turn to coat and refrigerate for about 8 hours.

2. Put potatoes, mushrooms, cauliflower, kidney beans, celery, onion, green beans and carrot in the slow cooker. Take meat out from the fridge, drain and add to slow cooker.

3. Add broth, sugar, parsley, salt, thyme, rosemary, marjoram, pepper, and the remaining garlic. Cover and cook for about 8 hours.

4. Then put cornstarch and water in a bowl, stir until smooth, add to soup and cook for about 30 minutes. When ready you can serve with rice. Enjoy!

Nutrition Information Per Serving: Calories377kcal; Fat12g; Carbohydrate44g; Protein22g

Keto Bacon Cheeseburger Soup
Comforting and cheesy! You need to try this.

Prep Time: 5 minutes

Cook Time: 15 minutes

Serves: 6

Ingredients

1 pound lean ground beef

1/2 can fire-roasted tomatoes

3 cups Beef Broth

1/4 cup crumbled bacon, cooked

1 tablespoon pickle jalapenos, chopped

2 teaspoons Worcestershire sauce

4 ounces cream cheese

1 cup sharp cheddar cheese, shredded

1/2 medium onion, cut

1 teaspoon salt

1/2 teaspoon pepper

1/2 teaspoon garlic powder

1 pickle spear, diced

Directions

1. Sauté ground beef on instant pot, add onion and cook well. Press cancel button.

2. Then add tomatoes, bacon, broth, garlic powder, Worcestershire sauce, jalapenos, salt and pepper. Stir and add cream cheese on top.

3. Press the soup button on instant pot and time for 15 minutes.

4. Serve and garnish with diced shredded cheddar and pickles

Nutrition Information Per Serving: Calories358kcal; *Fat*24g; *Carbohydrate*4.6g; *Protein*23.5g

Keto Jamaican Beef Stew

Exciting and comforting soup. Encumbered with vegetables.

Prep Time: 15 minutes

Cook Time: 4 hours

Serves: 6

Ingredients

2 pounds stew beef, cut and seasoned

¼ cup canola oil

3 pounds potatoes, cut

1 small bell pepper

2 Tablespoons tomato paste

1 Tablespoon thyme

 1 teaspoon hot sauce

1 teaspoon paprika, smoked

2 cups broth

2 teaspoons ginger, minced

1 Tablespoon garlic, minced

1 teaspoon all spice

2 bay leaves

3 Onions diced

3 Large carrots, cut

Salt and pepper to taste

Directions

1. In a pot on medium heat, add stew beef, fry until brown and add to slow cooker.

2. Put onion, onions, all spice, bell pepper, bay leaf, hot sauce, garlic, and thyme in a pot, stir and cook for about 3 minutes.

3. Put tomato paste, and bouillon. Stir and add broth. Boil and pour into the slow cooker where the beef is, add carrot and potatoes with salt.

4. Cook on high for about 4 hours. When ready, turn off and serve with bread

Nutrition Information Per Serving: Calories440kcal*; Fat21g; Carbohydrate16g; Protein44g*

Keto Easy Cheeseburger Soup

Easy soul reviving soup for you

Prep Time: 5 minutes

Cook Time: 25 minutes

Serves: 4

Ingredients

4 slices bacon, cut into pieces

2 cup beef broth

2 tablespoon butter, unsalted

1 lb. ground beef

2 tablespoon tomato paste

1 tablespoon mustard, yellow

1/2 teaspoon garlic powder

1/4 teaspoon paprika, smoked

6 ounce cheddar cheese, shredded

1/4 cup heavy whipping cream

1/4 teaspoon pepper

4 ounce cream cheese, softened

Salt

Directions

1. Cook bacon over medium heat until brown for about 8 minutes. Then pour bacon into a sieve to drain oil.

2. Add butter to pan to melt, put ground beef and cook well. Add cream cheese, garlic powder, tomato paste, smoked paprika, mustard, pepper, and salt.

3. Add beef broth and cream and boil on low heat. Put cheese and boil until smooth for about 7 minutes.

4. Then add bacon, turn off heat and let it cool for about 10 minutes to become thick and serve.

Nutrition Information Per Serving: Calories783kcal; *Fat66g; Carbohydrate4g; Protein40g*

Keto Beef Cabbage Soup

So filling! Soul reviving soup, you will like this.

Prep Time: 15 minutes

Cook Time: 20 minutes

Serves: 8

Ingredients

2 tablespoons olive oil

1 pound 500g rib eye, cut

1 stalk celery, sliced

1 green cabbage, chopped

6 cups beef broth

2 teaspoons dried thyme

2 teaspoons dried rosemary

2 teaspoons garlic powder

4 cloves garlic, minced

2 large carrots, diced

1 large onion chopped

3 tablespoons parsley, chopped

Salt to taste

Black pepper to taste

Directions

1. Put beef in the heated oil on medium heat, and fry until brown. Put onion cook for about 4 minutes.

2. Then put carrots and celery, stir frequently for about 4 minutes also and add cabbage, cook until softened for about 5 minutes.

3. Stir in garlic, broth, dried thyme and rosemary, parsley, and garlic powder. Stir and boil under low heat with lid on.

4. Boil for about 15 minutes and season with pepper and salt.

5. Serve when ready with parsley if you want. Enjoy!

Nutrition Information Per Serving: Calories177kcal; *Fat*11g; *Carbohydrate*4g; *Protein*12g

Keto Rogan Josh and Lamb Soup
Highly juicy and tasty for a cold night

Prep Time: 10 minutes

Cook Time: 45 minutes

Serves: 4

Ingredients

500 grams lamb, diced

1/2 red capsicum, diced

2 tablespoons butter

400 gram can tomatoes, crushed

1/2 lemon, juiced

1/2 cup chicken stock

1/2 teaspoon ground cardamom

1/2 teaspoon ground cloves

1 teaspoon cinnamon

1/2 tablespoon cayenne pepper

3/4 tablespoon paprika, smoked

1.5 tablespoons cumin heaped

1.5 tablespoons ground coriander heaped

1 teaspoon garlic paste

1/2 teaspoon ginger powder

1/2 onion, diced

Rogan Josh Spice Mix

1 cup plain yoghurt

2 teaspoons dried mint

Directions

1. Mix all spices in a bowl and set aside, melt butter on a medium heat in a large pot, add onion, garlic paste, and capsicum. Cook for about 2 minutes.

2. Put lamb, fry and stir frequently. When brown add the spices mixed in a bowl and stir well for about 2 minute until well coated.

3. Put chicken stock, tinned tomatoes, and the lemon juice and mix well. Boil for about 20 minutes with lid on and on low heat.

4. Mix mint and yoghurt well in a bowl and set aside. Open lid and boil for about 25 minutes until thickened to you desire and turn off heat.

5. Serve soup and enjoy with fresh coriander, cauliflower rice, and the mixed mint.

Nutrition Information Per Serving: Calories521kcal; *Fat*41g; *Carbohydrate*13g; *Protein*28

Keto Beef Barley Soup

Delicious and tasty, so comforting for you

Prep Time: 15 minutes

Cook Time: 1 hour 30 minutes

Serves: 8

Ingredients

1 ½ pounds stew meat

2 tablespoons oil

10 mushrooms, divided

1 onion, sliced

1 carrot, cut

1 stalk celery, slice

8 cloves garlic, minced

6 cups beef broth

1 cup water

2 bay leaves

½ teaspoon dried thyme

1 large potato, shredded

2/3 cup pearl barley

10 mushrooms, divided

1 onion, sliced

1 carrot, cut

1 stalk celery, slice

8 cloves garlic, minced

Salt and pepper

Directions

1. Heat oil in a pot, season the stew meat with salt a pepper and add to the oil, fry until brown for about 3 minutes. Take meat out into a plate and set side.

2. Add oil to pan and fry mushroom to brown for about 2 minutes and turn mushroom into same the plate the meat is.

3. Add oil to pan, when hot put carrot, onion, and celery. Cook for about 5 minutes and add garlic. Cook this for about 30 seconds.

4. Pour in the mushrooms and stew meat, bay leaves, beef broth, water, and dried thyme. Cook for about 16 minutes with lid on.

5. Put potatoes and barley and press the slow cook bottom and time to 1 hour. Seasoning with salt and pepper.

6. Serve with chopped parsley and a loaf of crusty bread if desired.

Nutrition Information Per Serving: Calories274kcal; *Fat*8.3g; *Carbohydrate*25g; *Protein*25.6g

Keto Beef with Bacon and Mushroom Soup

Flavored and tasty soup. Enjoy!

Prep Time: 10 minutes

Cook Time 35 minutes

Serves: 6

Ingredients

4 Slices Bacon, Sliced

3 Pounds Beef Stew Meat

3 Carrots, Chopped

8 Ounces Baby Bell Mushrooms, Sliced

2 Cups Beef Broth

1 teaspoon Salt

1/2 Onion, Diced

1/2 teaspoon Dried Thyme

Flour

Directions

1. Sauté bacon until crispy and bring out to drain on paper towels. Keep aside.

2. Put beef stew meat in a bowl and add salt then fry in the same oil used to fry bacon until brown. After frying put the beef in a plate.

3. Press cancel button, after adding beef, onion, mushroom, thyme, carrots, and broth to pot, place lid and set to pressure cook for about 35 minutes.

4. Hit the cancel button and let it cool for about 10 minutes add stir well. Serve and garnish with the cooked bacon that was kept aside.

5. Enjoy!

Nutrition Information Per Serving: Calories310kcal; *Fat*12g; *Carbohydrate*5g; *Protein*46g

Beef barley soup

Keto Indian Ground Beef Soup

Easy and tasty soup that will become your favorite.

Prep Time: 15 minutes

Cook Time 10 minutes

Serves: 4

Ingredients

1 cup frozen peas, frozen

4 pieces cinnamon sticks

4 pods cardamom

1 pound ground beef

1/2 teaspoon cayenne pepper

1/2 teaspoon ground coriander

1/2 teaspoon cumin

1 cup onion, sliced

1 tablespoon ginger, minced

1 tablespoon garlic

1/2 teaspoon turmeric

1 teaspoon masala

1/4 cup water

1 teaspoon salt

Directions

1. Hit the sauté button, and add oil to pot when hot, put the cardamom and the cinnamon sticks for about

2. Then put garlic, onions, and ginger. Cook for about 5 minutes and stir in the ground beef and boil for about 4 minutes.

3. Put water and spices and cook on high pressure for about 5 minutes with lid on. After 5 minutes put the peas.

4. Soup is ready.

Nutrition Information Per Serving: Calories334kcal*; Fat20g; Carbohydrate6g; Protein29g*

Keto Irish Lamb Soup

So nourishing and delicious. You need to try this.

Prep Time: 15 minutes

Cook Time 2 hours

Serves: 6

Ingredients

2 1/2 lb. lamb shoulder, chopped

4 slices bacon, sliced

4 cups chicken beef

2 lb. potatoes, peeled and sliced

1 turnip, chopped

6 medium carrots, sliced

2 onions, cut

1 teaspoon dried thyme

Salt

Pepper

Directions

1. Put bacon in an oven on medium heat, cook for about 4 minutes. When crispy put bacon in a paper towel.

2. Add salt and pepper to the lamb and put in the oven to brown and remove to a plate.

3. In the oven put onion, when brown add the lamb, broth and dried thyme. Boil for some minutes and reduce heat to simmer for about 90 minutes.

4. Then put turnip, carrots, and potatoes. Cook for about 20 minutes.

5. Enjoy!

Nutrition Information Per Serving: Calories: 458kcal*; Fat*17g*; Carbohydrate*37g*; Protein*36g

Keto Moroccan Lamb Soup
Hearty and filling. You won't regret cooking

Prep Time: 20 minutes

Cook Time 1 hours 50 minutes

Serves: 4

Ingredients

1 tablespoon olive oil

2 large lamb shanks

1/2 teaspoon ground cinnamon

400g can diced tomatoes

1/2 cup dried green lentils, washed

2 celery stalks, chopped

2 teaspoons ground cumin

2 medium carrots, chopped

2 teaspoons ground coriander

1/2 teaspoon ground ginger

1 tablespoon beef stock powder

1/4 cup parsley, chopped

1 onion, sliced

2 garlic cloves, minced

Directions

1. Put oil in a pot on high heat, when hot put shanks and cook for about 8 minutes turning frequently. Remove and put in a plate

2. Put onion, carrot, celery and garlic to the oil and cook for about 5 minutes, then put coriander, cinnamon, cumin, and ginger.

3. After 1 minutes put the cooked shanks, tomatoes, water, and stock powder then boil. Decrease heat to boil gently for about 30 minutes.

4. Take shanks out and remove the bones, shred lamb and add back to soup with parsley. Simmer for about 5 minutes.

5. Enjoy.

Nutrition Information Per Serving: Calories: 245kcal*; Fat*17.8g*; Carbohydrate*21.4g*Protein*36.5g

Keto Kerala Lamb Soup

A coconut meal full of flavor. Try this.

Prep Time: 10 minutes

Cook Time 30 minutes

Serves: 3

Ingredients

200g Boneless lamb

200ml Coconut Milk

2 tablespoon Coconut Oil

2 teaspoon ginger and garlic paste

50g Onion

2 ginger cloves

2 bay leaves

1 green chilly

300ml water

10g Coriander

2 teaspoon ginger and garlic paste

50g Onion

2 cloves

15 curry leaves

1/2 teaspoon coriander powder

1/2 teaspoon red chili Powder

Salt

Pepper

Directions

1. Season lamb with chili powder, coriander powder, ginger and garlic paste, salt, and pepper.

2. Heat some of the coconut oil and fry lamb till brown and stir in cloves, bay leaves, green chili and cinnamon stick.

3. Add onion, and water. Cook for about 30 minutes with lid on.

4. Open and put coconut milk and curry leaves and boil for about 3 minutes. Then add coriander and turn off heat.

5. Serve and enjoy!

Nutrition Information Per Serving: Calories: 284kcal*; Fat20g; Carbohydrate4gProtein22g*

Keto Ground Beef Taco Soup

Yummy and soul filling. Let's cook.

Prep Time: 10 minutes

Cook Time 20 minutes

Serves: 8

Ingredients

1 pound ground beef

1/2 cup onion, sliced

2 cloves garlic, shredded

1 tablespoon ground cumin

1 teaspoon chili powder

8 ounce package cream cheese, softened

2 cans beef broth

2 cans diced tomatoes and green chilies

1/2 cup heavy cream

1/2 cup onion, sliced

2 cloves garlic, shredded

1 tablespoon ground cumin

1 teaspoon chili powder

8 ounce package cream cheese, softened

2 teaspoons salt

Directions

1. Cook ground beef, garlic, and onion over high heat. When brown and crunchy for about 7 minutes, remove oil and put chili powder and cumin.

2. After 2 minutes, put cheese and stir frequently to mix, put broth, heavy cream, diced tomatoes, and salt. Cook for about 10 minutes.

3. Season with and pepper if needed and taco seasoning mix.

4. Enjoy!

Nutrition Information Per Serving: Calories: 288kcal; *Fat*24g; *Carbohydrate*5.4 g*Protein*13.4 g

Keto Cabbage and Corned Beef Soup
Delicious and yummy. Try this

Prep Time: 20minutes

Cook Time 50 minutes

Serves: 10

Ingredients

6 tablespoons butter

1 ½ teaspoon mustard seed, toasted

3 pounds corned beef, diced

2 tablespoons tomato paste

4 cups cabbage, chopped

5 turnips, diced

1 medium onion, cut

2 celery stalks, cut

1 fennel bulb, cut

2 cloves garlic, crushed

½ teaspoon salt

Ground black pepper

½ cup parsley, cut

Bay leaf

Fennel fronds, diced

1 fresh lemon, juiced

Directions

1. Put butter in pot and sauté onion for about 10 minutes. Put garlic, celery stalks, and fennel, cook for about 6 minutes.

2. Put mustard seed in the center of the pot, cook and stir for about 2 minutes. Add water to pot and stir. Then put tomato paste, bay leaf, corned beef, turnips, cabbage, salt and pepper.

3. Add water if need and cook for about 30 minutes with lid on

4. Open lid to vent add fennel fronds, parsley, and juice stir and turn off heat.

5. Enjoy soup.

Nutrition Information Per Serving: Calories: 331kcal*; Fat*24g*; Carbohydrate*9.2g *Protein*20g

PORK RECIPES

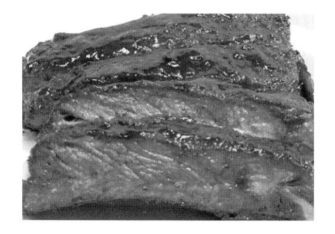

Keto Southwestern Pork Soup

Hearty soup that warms up your belly. So yummy

Prep Time: 10minutes

Cook Time 25 minutes

Serves: 10

Ingredients

1 pound pork Shoulder, cooked and sliced

6 ounces button mushrooms

2 cups pork bone broth

2 cup chicken broth

½ cup strong coffee

¼ cup tomato paste

2 teaspoons chili powder

2 teaspoons cumin

1 teaspoon garlic, crushed

½ jalapeno, sliced

½ onion

½ green bell pepper, sliced

½ red bell pepper, sliced

½ lime, juiced

½ teaspoon salt

½ teaspoon pepper

1 teaspoon paprika

1 teaspoon oregano

¼ teaspoon cinnamon

2 small bay leaves

Directions

1. Heat UP oil, Put all veggies and cook them slightly and add spices for about 3 minutes. Keep aside

2. Boil bone and chicken broth with coffee on low heat. Put pork and mushrooms. Then add the cooked veggies with spices into broth and stir well.

3. Cook for about 15minutes with lid on.

4. Enjoy!

Nutrition Information Per Serving: Calories: 386kcal; Fat28.9g; Carbohydrate6.4g Protein19.9g

Keto Taco Soup with Mexican Pulled Pork

Super tasty and super healthy. Just in 15 minutes

Prep Time: 5minutes

Cook Time 15 minutes

Serves: 4

Ingredients

1 tablespoon olive oil

1 onion, chopped

1 red bell pepper, chopped

1 can red kidney beans

1 can sweet corn

2 garlic cloves, crushed

2 teaspoon oregano

2 teaspoon cumin

1 teaspoon paprika

2 cups Mexican pulled pork, shredded

680g tomatoes, crushed

4 cups chicken broth

Salt

Pepper

Directions

1. In a pot add oil and cook pulled pork for about 1 minute on high heat until brown. Then put into a plate.

2. Put onion and garlic into oil and cook for about 2 minutes, put the bell pepper, pulled pork, red kidney beans, sweet corn, oregano, cumin, paprika, tomatoes, and chicken broth .

3. Stir well and boil on low heat for about 5 minutes. Then season with salt and pepper.

4. Serve and garnish with parsley.

Nutrition Information Per Serving: Calories: 398kcal*; Fat2g; Carbohydrate63.9g Protein23.8g*

Keto Pork Chops with Onion Soup Mix

This soup is super tasty and fast. You will like it

Prep Time: 5minutes

Cook Time 15 minutes

Serves: 6

Ingredients

6 pork chops

Olive oil

1/2 cup water

2 pounds potatoes, peeled and sliced

6 carrots, sliced

1 packet onion soup mix

1 large onion, chopped

Salt &Pepper

Parsley

Directions

1. Fry pork chops and put the soup mix. Stir well for about 5 minutes.

2. Put water, potatoes, carrots, and onion. Mix well and cook for 5 more minutes.

3. Put salt and pepper to taste, add more water if needed and boil for about 3 minutes on high heat.

4. Serve and sprinkle parsley on it. Enjoy!

Nutrition Information Per Serving: Calories: 391kcal*; Fat*16g*; Carbohydrate*29g *Protein*32g

Keto Kale and Sausage Soup

Hearty, tasty, and creamy soup for you.

Prep Time: 10minutes

Cook Time 20 minutes

Serves: 3

Ingredients

1 pound organic Italian sausage

½ cup pancetta, chopped

2 cups organic heavy cream

2 cups chicken broth

2 cups kale, chopped

1 tablespoon garlic, crushed

½ cup onion, chopped

½ teaspoon red pepper flakes

½ teaspoon ground black pepper

½ teaspoon Italian seasoning

Salt

Directions

1. Over medium heat cook the Italian sausage, onion, and pancetta for about 5 minutes.

2. Put chicken broth, garlic, black pepper, heavy cream, red pepper flakes, and Italian seasoning.

3. Stir and boil on low heat for about 10 minutes with lid on

4. Add salt to taste if needed, and kale. Cook for about 5 minutes.

5. Soup is ready.

Nutrition Information Per Serving: Calories470kcal; *Fat*45g; *Carbohydrate*3g *Protein*4g

Kale soup

Keto Asian Pork Soup
Super spicy and soul filling, try this

Prep Time: 20minutes

Cook Time; 30minutes

Serves: 4

Ingredients

12 ounces boneless pork, cut

3 cans chicken broth

2 tablespoons dry sherry

2 tablespoons soy sauce

2 cups Chinese cabbage, sliced

2 cups mushrooms, sliced

2 cloves garlic, crushed

2 teaspoons ginger, grated

¼ teaspoon red pepper, crushed

1 green onion, sliced

Directions

1. Put oil in a pot on medium heat, fry pork for about 5 minutes and keep aside.

2. Put garlic and mushrooms in the oil, add broth, soy sauce, red pepper, sherry, and ginger.

3. Boil for about 10 minutes and put pork, onion and cabbage. Cook for about 15 minutes on low heat.

4. Enjoy!

Nutrition Information Per Serving: Calories140kcal*; Fat*3g*; Carbohydrate*10g *Protein*16g

Keto Cabbage with Chicken and Pork Soup
Comforting and spicy soup for you.

Prep Time: 15minutes

Cook Time; 30minutes

Serves: 8

Ingredients

1 cabbage, sliced

15oz. chicken breasts

6 oz. lean pork

1 chicken bullion

3 carrots, chopped

1 yellow pepper, sliced

2 cloves garlic, crushed

2 bay leaves

1/4 teaspoon cumin

1.5oz. brandy

8 cups of water

2 whites leeks, sliced

Salt

Pepper

Directions

1. Cook chicken breast and pork in a pot on high heat with spices for about 10 minutes.

2. Put carrot, onion, leek, garlic and cabbage and boil for about 5 minutes.

3. Add chicken bouillon, yellow pepper, bay leaves, cumin, and brandy.

4. Boil for about 7 minutes and add salt and pepper to taste.

5. Soup is ready.

Nutrition Information Per Serving: Calories255.2kcal*; Fat*7.4g*; Carbohydrate*12.5g *Protein*31.7g

Keto Kimchi and Pork Soup
It's yummy. You need to try it.

Prep Time: 5 minutes

Cook Time; 20minutes

Serves: 4

Ingredients

1 lb. ground pork

1/2 cup kimchi juice

2 cups kimchi, chopped

4 cups beef broth

4 onions, diced

4 cloves garlic, crushed

1 tablespoon ginger, grated

<u>Directions</u>

1. Over medium heat, fry pork and stir frequently about 7 minutes.

2. When brown add garlic, ginger, and onions after 2 minutes or when cooked add kimchi, beef broth, kimchi juice.

3. Let it boil well on low heat for about 10 minutes

4. Serve and enjoy.

Nutrition Information Per Serving: Calories325.2kcal*; Fat24g; Carbohydrate5g Protein22g*

Keto Peppers, Spinach and Sausage Soup
Spicy and delightful soup for you

Prep Time: 10 minutes

Cook Time; 35 minutes

Serves: 6

Ingredients

2 tablespoon olive oil

1 lb. pork sausage

6 cups organic chicken stock

3 celery stalks, diced

1/2 teaspoon ground cinnamon

2 red pepper, diced

1 teaspoon dried basil

1 teaspoon dried oregano

1 teaspoon dried rosemary

1.5 teaspoon chili powder

1 teaspoon ground cumin

2 cups spinach

1 cup cheese, shredded

Salt to taste

Black pepper to taste

Directions

1. Add oil to pot when hot add sausage and cook until golden brown for about 5 minutes. Then break pork into smaller pieces with spoon and set aside

2. In a pot, put red pepper, oregano, celery, rosemary, basil, chili powder, cinnamon, and cumin. Season with salt and black pepper and stir continuously for about 6 minutes.

3. When soft put chicken stock and boil for about 20 minutes. Then put spinach and cook for about 5 minutes.

4. Serve and garnish with shredded cheese. Enjoy!

Nutrition Information Per Serving: Calories301.2kcal*; Fat20g; Carbohydrate3.9 g Protein16g*

Zuppa Toscana Keto Meatball Soup with Sausage and Kale
Yummy and easy soup for you

Prep Time: 15 minutes

Cook Time; 45 minutes

Serves: 8

Ingredients

2 lbs. pork, minced

8 cups bone broth

1 medium onion, diced

3, garlic cloves, minced

1/2 teaspoon sea salt

1 teaspoon dried sage

1 teaspoon dried thyme

1/2 teaspoon ground allspice

2 tsp Italian seasoning

1/2 tsp freshly squeezed lemon juice

2 teaspoon fresh rosemary, chopped

1 cup parmesan, grated

3/4 cup heavy cream

2 cups torn kale leaves

2/3 cup dry white wine

2 bay leaves

Sea salt

Black pepper

Red pepper flakes, crushed

Directions

1. Season the minced pork with sage, salt, allspice, and thyme in a bowl, mix well and roll to form balls.

2. In a pot on high heat, add broth, onion, lemon juice, garlic, bay leaves, Italian seasoning, and rosemary. Boil well for about 30 minutes.

3. Drain solid from broth and put back to heat. Add the cream and Parmesan stir and boil for about 5 minutes.

4. Then put wine, kale and the uncooked meatballs and cook for about 10 minutes. Season with salt and pepper to taste.

5. Serve and garnish with red pepper flakes.

Nutrition Information Per Serving: Calories429.2kcal*; Fat*33g*; Carbohydrate*5g
*Protein*28g

Keto Italian Wedding Broth Soup
Easy soup that's perfect for you. So yummy!

Prep Time: 10 minutes

Cook Time; 20 minutes

Serves: 6

Ingredients

3 cups cauliflower rice

1/2 pound ground beef

1/2 pound ground pork

10 cups chicken broth

1/2 cup almond flour

8 ounces spinach leaves, chopped

1/2 cup diced carrots, diced

1 cup parmesan cheese, grated

3 eggs

3 garlic cloves, grated

1/4 cup fresh parsley, shared

2 teaspoons dried

Salt to taste

Pepper to taste

Directions

1. In a pot, put in egg, basil, almond flour, salt and pepper. Stir and boil for few minutes and put the pork and ground beef and stir gently.

2. Boil chicken broth in another pot and use a small scooper for the cooked beef and pork to form meatballs and put them in the broth.

3. Then put parmesan cheese rind and carrot, boil for about 10 minutes, put spinach and cauliflower rice and cook for about 7 minutes.

4. Whisk the eggs and stir it in, cook for few minutes on low heat. Serve and garnish with parsley and some grated parmesan cheese.

Nutrition Information Per Serving: Calories326kcal*; Fat21g; Carbohydrate8g Protein26g*

Keto Pumpkin Pork Sausage Soup
So sweet so nourishing. You will love it.

Prep Time: 15 minutes

Cook Time; 20 minutes

Serves: 6

Ingredients

4 cups chicken broth

1 pound pork sausage, uncooked

1 onion, diced

2 garlic cloves, crushed

1 tablespoon Italian seasoning

1 15 ounce can pumpkin

4 cups chicken broth

1 can coconut milk

1 cup water

Sea salt

Directions

1. Fry sausage, set aside, sauté onion and garlic then add Italian seasoning and salt.

2. Add pumpkin, stir and cook well.

3. Putin the broth, stir and simmer for about 30 minutes.

4. Add half of the coconut milk and water and boil on low heat for 15 minute.

5. Put salt and pepper to taste and serve. Garnish second half coconut milk

Nutrition Information Per Serving: Calories440 kcal; *Fat*38g; *Carbohydrate*10g *Protein*14g

Keto Instant Pot Cabbage Rolls Pork Soup

Flavored soup for you. So easy

Prep Time: 15 minutes

Cook Time; 45 minutes

Serves: 6

Ingredients

3 tablespoons Olive Oil

1 1/2 Pound Ground Pork

5 Cups Beef Broth

6 Ounce can tomato paste

28 Ounce can tomatoes, diced

1 cabbage, chopped

1 tablespoon dried oregano

2 teaspoons Fresh Thyme, chopped

1/4 cup fresh parsley, chopped

1 onion, Chopped

4 garlic, minced

Sour Cream

Salt to Taste

Pepper to taste

Directions

1. Sauté meat and onions for about 2 minutes on instant pot, put garlic and cook for about 1 minutes.

2. Stir in Beef Broth, tomato paste, diced tomatoes, cabbage, dried oregano, Fresh thyme, and fresh parsley.

3. Stir and press the soup button, cover and time to 35minutes

4. Release steam for about 20 minutes and turn off heat.

5. Serve and top with the sour cream

Nutrition Information Per Serving: Calories503kcal*; Fat*31g*; Carbohydrate*11g *Protein*44g

Keto Pork Watercress Soup

So easy so tasty. Perfect for you

Prep Time: 10 minutes

Cook Time; 20 minutes

Serves: 4

Ingredients

1.25 lb. fresh pork loin filet, chopped

3 cups watercress

3 cups chicken broth

1 tablespoon olive oil

8 oz. mushrooms, sliced

1 inch piece ginger, minced

1 teaspoon garlic, minced

2 scallions, chopped

Directions

1. Fry pork with oil until brown and pieces for about 5 minutes. Put garlic and ginger and cook for 1 minutes.

2. Put chicken broth and mushrooms. Boil for 10 minutes until pork and mushrooms are cooked.

3. Add watercress and scallions, cook for about 2 minutes.

4. Enjoy!

Nutrition Information Per Serving: Calories251kcal; *Fat*13.5g; *Carbohydrate*7g *Protein*27g

Keto Instant Pot Pork Soup

Enjoy a healthy soup that's comforting

Prep Time: 12 minutes

Cook Time; 1 hour 20 minutes

Serves: 6

Ingredients

1.5 lb. potatoes, cut

3 stalks celery, sliced

8 oz. mushrooms, sliced

1 ½ cup chicken broth

2 teaspoon garlic

1 teaspoon thyme dried

1/2 teaspoon garlic powder

1 teaspoon onion powder

1 teaspoon white pepper

2 tablespoon oil

3 carrots, sliced

1 onion, diced

1 teaspoon salt

1 teaspoon pepper

Directions

1. Season the pork, add oil to instant pot and press the sauté button. Put in the pork and fry well and stir continuously.

2. Add carrot, onion, and celery. Sauté for few minutes and put mushrooms, potatoes, garlic powder, onion powder, and white pepper.

3. Stir and add the stock. Place lid, seal, add set on manual for 25 minutes.

4. Release heat naturally, serve and enjoy!

Nutrition Information Per Serving: Calories142kcal*; Fat*5g*; Carbohydrate*18g *Protein*5g

Keto Instant Pot Mexican Pork Soup

Tasty and comforting soup. You will like it

Prep Time: 10 minutes

Cook Time; 30 minutes

Serves: 12

Ingredients

36 ounces pork shoulder, shredded

2 cups pumpkin, cooked

6 cups chicken broth

6 tablespoon pork lard

1 cup cilantro, chopped

1 lime, cut

4 avocados, diced

1 cup canned green chili, chopped

2 teaspoon ground cumin

2 teaspoon garlic powder

1 teaspoon paprika, smoked

1 teaspoon sea salt

4 cups kale, chopped

1 onion, diced

Directions

1. Mix cumin, paprika, garlic powder, and salt in a bowl

2. Sauté pork lard, put onion, pork shoulder, spices mixed in the bowl, green chili, pumpkin, and broth.

3. Close lid and set on high heat for 30 minutes.

4. Then put kale and turn off heat.

5. Top with avocado and cilantro, garnish with lime and enjoy!

Nutrition Information Per Serving: Calories340 kcal*; Fat23g; Carbohydrate*13g *Protein*24g

BROTH RECIPES

Keto Turmeric and Chicken Bone Broth Soup

So tasty. You'll love this!

Prep Time: 10 minutes

Cook Time; 20minutes

Serves: 4

Ingredients

2 tablespoon butter

6 cups chicken bone broth

1 lb. ground turkey, crumbled

1/2 teaspoon ground coriander

1/4 teaspoon ground cinnamon

1/4 teaspoon cayenne pepper

1/4 cup cilantro, chopped

6 cloves garlic

1 piece turmeric root, minced

3/4 teaspoon ground turmeric

1 bunch kale, diced

1 onion, chopped

1 tablespoon ginger, grated

1/2 lemon, juiced

Black pepper

Salt

Directions

1. Heat butter and put kale, and onion cook for about 4 minutes, then add ginger, and garlic.

2. Cook for about 2 minutes and stir in ground and minced turmeric, boil for about 1 minute.

3. Stir and add turkey, cinnamon, coriander, black pepper, cilantro, cayenne, and 1 teaspoon salt.

4. Cook well for about 7 minutes, add half cup of broth and stir well using spoon to gather all browned bits, then add all broth.

5. Boil for about 10 minutes on low heat, add kale leaves and boil for about 1 minutes. Add lemon juice and salt and pepper to taste. Enjoy!

Nutrition Information Per Serving: Calories372kcal*; Fat26g; Carbohydrate7g Protein30g*

Keto Beef, Pork with Tough Broth Soup

So tasty! You will sure get that taste you desire.

Prep Time: 2 minutes

Cook Time; 35 minutes

Serves: 6

Ingredients

2.5 liter broth (mixture of beef shank and ham hock broth and coconut oil)

500 gram meat, cooked

Broccoli, chopped

Brussel sprouts, chopped

Carrots, chopped

Cauliflower, chopped

Leeks, chopped

2 bay leaves

1.5 liter water

Pepper

Chili

Cumin

Garlic powder

Italian herbs

2 tablespoon Salt

Directions

1. Boil water, add meat and broth on medium heat.

2. Put broccoli, Brussel sprouts, carrots, cauliflower, leeks, bay leaves, garlic powder and chili.

3. Boil for about 5 minutes and add cumin, pepper, Italian herbs and salt.

4. Cook with lid on for about 30 minutes.

5. Serve and enjoy.

Nutrition Information Per Serving: Calories93.1kcal; Fat7.5g; Carbohydrate0.1g Protein6.3g

Keto Buffalo and Chicken Broth Soup
Delicious meal for cold night. Enjoy!

Prep Time: 10 minutes

Cook Time; 25 minutes

Serves: 8

<u>Ingredients</u>

2 tablespoons butter

6 cups chicken broth

2/3 cup hot sauce

1 rotisserie chicken, shredded

3 cups cheddar cheese

2 cups heavy cream

4 ribs celery, chopped

1/2 of an onion, chopped

3 garlic cloves, chopped

2 tablespoons ranch dressing mix

Directions

1. Add butter to pan when hot put onion, celery, and garlic. Fry until soft.

2. In another pot add chicken broth, and stir in the fried vegetables, put hot sauce, ranch dressing mix, and shredded chicken.

3. Cook for about 15minutes on high heat. When ready turn off heat and add cream.

4. Enjoy!

Nutrition Information Per Serving: Calories630kcal*; Fat53g; Carbohydrate6g Protein32g*

Keto Lemon Chicken Broth Soup

So delicious you can't resist

Prep Time: 15minutes

Cook Time; 30 minutes

Serves: 6

Ingredients

1 tablespoon olive oil

10 cups chicken broth

1 cup whole wheat orzo

3 cups rotisserie chicken, shredded

1 handful of fresh spinach

1 1/2 teaspoons salt

Freshly ground pepper

3 carrots, diced

1 onion, diced

3 cloves garlic, minced

3 eggs

4 lemon, juiced

Directions

1. Fry carrot with oil, add garlic, and onion. Fry for about 10 minutes.

2. Add broth, orzo, and chicken. Beat eggs and lemon together, add to soup gradually.

4. Add spinach and salt and pepper to taste. Enjoy!

Keto Hamburger Cabbage Beef Soup

Hearty and creamy. You would love this.

Prep Time: 10 minutes

Cook Time; 20 minutes

Serves: 6

Ingredients

1 pound ground beef

6 cups beef broth

2 teaspoons cumin

1 tablespoon avocado oil

1 cup onion, chopped

8 cups cabbage, chopped

2 cups zucchini, pieced

1 14 ounce can diced tomatoes

1/2 teaspoon ground coriander

1 teaspoon garlic powder

1/2 teaspoon chili powder

12 ounce green chilies, diced

Directions

1. Fry beef with cumin, coriander, chili powder, garlic powder and salt.

2. Then put green chilies when beef is cooked.

3. Put in cabbage, zucchini and onion. Cook until soften.

4. Pour beef broth in the soup and boil for about 20 minutes.

5. Enjoy!

Nutrition Information Per Serving: Calories584kcal; *Fat17g; Carbohydrate80g Protein42g*

Keto Chicken Broth Soup
So creamy and comforting

Prep Time: 10 minutes

Cook Time; 35 minutes

Serves: 6

Ingredients

1 chicken breast, diced

1/4 cup oil

4 cups chicken broth

1/2 cup jicama, chopped

1/4 cup cauliflower rice, blended into pieces

1 1/2 teaspoon masala

1onion, chopped

2 stalks celery, chopped

Salt to taste

Black pepper to taste

1 pinch dried thyme

1/2 cup coconut milk

Directions

1. Cook celery and onion in the heated oil, put masala and cook for about 5 minutes.

2. Put chicken broth, stir and boil for about 10 minutes.

3. Put jicama, chicken, cauliflower rice, thyme, salt and pepper. Cook for about 20 minutes.

4. Serve and top with coconut milk. Enjoy!

Nutrition Information Per Serving: Calories171kcal; *Fat*13g; *Carbohydrate*3.8g *Protein*7.9g

Keto Slow Cooker Low Carb Beef Broth Soup
So tasty and comforting. You would like this.

Prep Time: 15 minutes

Cook Time; 4 hours

Serves: 12

Ingredients

3 pounds ground beef

3 cups beef broth

3/4 cup red pepper, chopped

1 small jalapeno, chopped

24 ounces marinara sauce

14 ounces tomatoes, diced

4 tablespoon tomato paste

2 tablespoon cocoa powder

2 cups onion, chopped

4 cloves garlic, minced

1 tablespoon ground cumin

3 teaspoon chili powder

1 teaspoon dried oregano

Salt and pepper to taste

Directions

1. Fry ground beef until golden brown. Add garlic, onion, and dried oregano.

2. Then put soup into the slow cooker, add beef broth, red pepper and jalapeno.

3. Add marinara sauce, tomatoes, tomato paste, cocoa powder, ground cumin, and chili powder.

4. Stir well, close lid, set to cook on high for about 4 hours.

5. Serve and top with cheddar cheese if desired.

Nutrition Information Per Serving: Calories363kcal*; Fat26g; Carbohydrate9g Protein21g*

Keto Slow Cooker Zuppa Toscana Vegetable Broth Soup

Delicious meal that keeps you healthy

Prep Time: 10 minutes

Cook Time; 4 hours

Serves: 10

Ingredients

1 pound mild

1 tablespoon oil

1 medium onion, diced

3 garlic cloves, minced

1 large cauliflower head, diced

36 ounces vegetable stock

3 cups kale, chopped

¼ teaspoon red pepper flakes, crushed

1 tablespoon oil

1 medium onion, diced

3 garlic cloves, minced

½ cup heavy cream

1 teaspoon salt

½ teaspoon pepper

Directions

1. Fry the mild until brown and put in slow cooker, sauté onion and add to mild.

2. Add vegetable stock, crushed red pepper flakes, cauliflower florets, kale, salt and pepper to slow cooker.

3. Sir well and cook on high for about 4 hours.

4. Then add heavy cream, stir well and serve.

Nutrition Information Per Serving: Calories246kcal; *Fat*19g; *Carbohydrate*7g *Protein*14g

Keto Spinach Chicken Broth Soup
Yummy! You will like the taste

Prep Time: 10 minutes

Cook Time; 25 minutes

Serves: 4

Ingredients

1 ½ cups chicken broth

10 oz. spinach, chopped

3 tablespoon butter

2 tablespoon coconut flour

1 bunch of cilantro, minced

1 stick of celery

3 cups coconut milk

1 onion, minced

Salt

Pepper

Directions

1. Boil chicken broth, and spinach for few minutes until spinach is soften. Turn off the heat and let the mixture cool.

2. Blend mixture and set aside. Melt butter and add coconut flour, coconut milk, cilantro, celery, and onion.

3. Stir well and put in spinach mixture and cook well.

4. Serve and enjoy!

Nutrition Information Per Serving: Calories139kcal*; Fat*12g*; Carbohydrate* 4.6g *Protein*1.7g

Keto Roasted Red Pepper Chicken Broth Soup

A spicy and comforting taste for you.

Prep Time: 10 minutes

Cook Time; 40minutes

Serves: 12

Ingredients

2.5 lb. sweet peppers

2 cups chicken broth

2 scoops Chicken Bone Broth Collagen

2 cups heavy cream

1 lb. chopped cauliflower

Onion

Salt

Pepper

Directions

1. Roast the sweet peppers for about 30 minutes at 400 degrees on a baking sheet until brown.

2. Boil broth and cauliflower on high heat and add the bone broth collagen.

3. Blend roasted peppers, half of the boiled broth with cauliflower, and onion in a blender smoothly.

4. Pour back to pot and boil. Add salt a pepper to taste.

5. Serve and top with heavy cream if desired.

Nutrition Information Per Serving: Calories183kcal*; Fat*15g*; Carbohydrate*8g *Protein*4g

Keto French Onion and Beef Broth Soup
Full of flavor and so tasty. Enjoy!

Prep Time: 10 minutes

Cook Time; 25 minutes

Serves: 4

Ingredients

3 tablespoons butter

1 tablespoon Worcestershire sauce

4 cups beef broth

2 tablespoons fresh rosemary

1 cup mozzarella cheese, shredded

2 garlic cloves, crushed

2 small onions, sliced

1 teaspoon salt

1 teaspoon black pepper

Directions

1. Heat up butter to melt, add garlic and onion cook for about 7 minutes.

2. Put Worcestershire sauce, beef broth, rosemary, salt. And pepper.

3. Mix well and boil for about 10 minutes and serve.

4. Top with cheese and put under broiler until cheese are melted for about 7 minutes.

5. Enjoy!

Nutrition Information Per Serving: Calories180 kcal*; Fat*14g*; Carbohydrate*7g *Protein*9g

Keto Bacon Cheeseburger Beef Broth Soup
Super tasty and creamy, try this

Prep Time: 20 minutes

Cook Time; 60 minutes

Serves: 12

Ingredients

4 cups beef broth

1/3 cup dill pickles, chopped

8 slices bacon, cooked and pounded

2 tablespoons Dijon Mustard

1 ½ pounds ground beef

1 1/2 cups cheddar cheese, shredded

2 tablespoons Worcestershire sauce

2 tablespoons parsley, chopped

1 onion, diced

4 cloves garlic, minced

1 cup heavy cream

1 tomato, diced

Salt and black pepper to taste

Directions

1. Fry ground beef, garlic and onion for about few minutes until beef is cooked through.

2. Put beef broth, Dijon, pickles, tomato, Worcestershire sauce, parsley, black pepper and salt.

3. Stir well and boil for about 30 minutes. Then put heavy cream and cheddar cheese and boil on low heat for about 30 minutes.

4. Stir thoroughly and add bacon. Serve and enjoy!

Nutrition Information Per Serving: Calories306 kcal*; Fat*11g*; Carbohydrate*3g *Protein*13g

Keto Cheeseburger Chicken Broth Soup

So delicious and cheesy. Perfect for you.

Prep Time: 25 minutes

Cook Time; 20 minutes

Serves: 8

Ingredients

1 pound ground beef

2 cups chicken broth

1 tablespoon tomato paste

3/4 cup onion, minced

3/4 cup carrots, grated

3/4 cup celery, grated

3/4 cup cauliflower, grated

1 cup cream cheese, softened

2 cups cheddar cheese, shredded

2 cups milk

1 teaspoon creole seasoning

Salt and pepper to taste

Directions

1. Fry beef until brown for about 5 minutes, put onions, carrots, celery, and cauliflower.

2. Cook for about 5 minutes and put cheese, stir and let it melt, put tomato paste, and milk.

3. Put chicken broth, salt and pepper. Cook on low heat for about 5 minutes,

4. Serve and top shredded cheese and creole seasoning.

Nutrition Information Per Serving: Calories412 kcal*; Fat*32g*; Carbohydrate*8g *Protein*21g

Keto Avocado and Chicken Broth Soup
So comforting and tasty. You will ask for more.

Prep Time: 5 minutes

Cook Time; 20 minutes

Serves: 4

Ingredients

2 tablespoon olive oil

8 ounces avocados, diced

2 cups chicken breast, shredded and cooked

5 cups reduced sodium chicken broth

1 cups scallions, chopped

1 medium tomato, diced

1/3 cup cilantro, chopped

2 cloves garlic, minced

4 lime wedges

1/8 teaspoon cumin

Chili powder

Salt

Pepper

Directions

1. Heat up oil, put scallions and garlic. Cook for about 3 minutes and put tomatoes.

2. When soft add chicken broth, Chili powder, cilantro, and cumin. Boil on low heat for about 15 minutes.

3. Add salt and pepper to taste, share avocado and chicken breast in four bowls, and put soup in each bowl.

4. Top with lime wedge. Enjoy!

Nutrition Information Per Serving: Calories297kcal; *Fat*14g; *Carbohydrate*14.5g *Protein*31g

Keto Pumpkin Chicken Broth Soup

So easy and comforting. For you.

Prep Time: 10 minutes

Cook Time; 10 minutes

Serves: 6

Ingredients

15 oz. pumpkin puree

4 cups chicken broth

2 tablespoon chopped parsley

1/2 teaspoon garlic powder

1 teaspoon fresh thyme

1/2 cup heavy cream

1/4 cup sour cream

Salt and pepper

Directions

1. Boil chicken broth, pumpkin puree, garlic, thyme, salt, and pepper for about 10 minutes

2. Turn off heat, add heavy cream and serve.

3. Garnish with sour cream and parsley if desired.

4. Enjoy!

Nutrition Information Per Serving: Calories120kcal*; Fat*9g*; Carbohydrate*7g *Protein*2g

The End

Made in United States
Orlando, FL
24 February 2022

15125606R00085